FIFTY SHADES
OF
MANDALA
COLORING BOOK

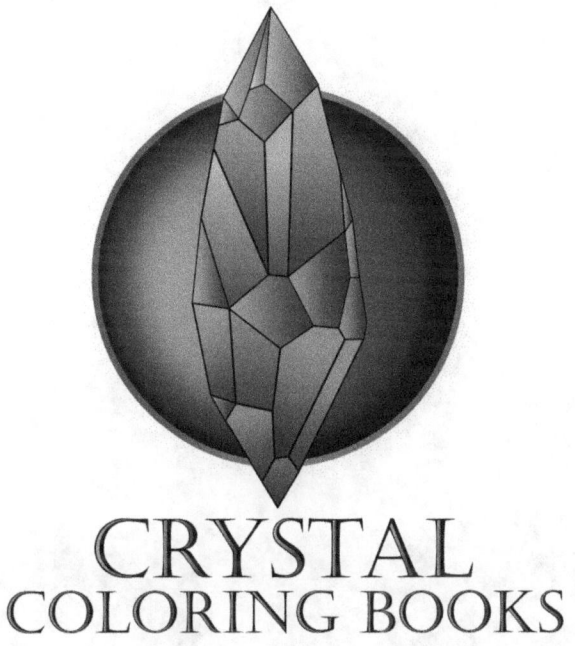

CRYSTAL
COLORING BOOKS

ISBN: 9781087237367

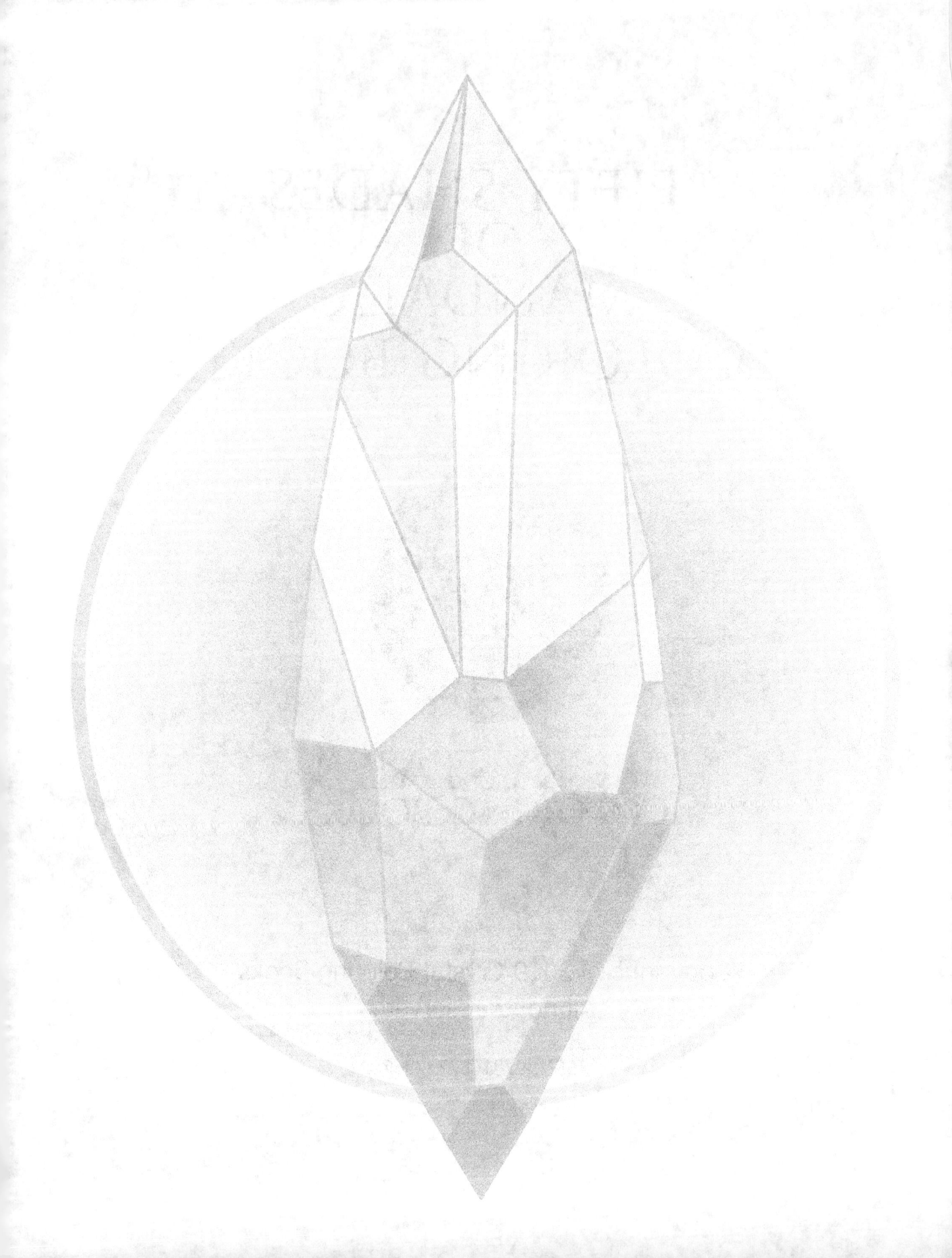

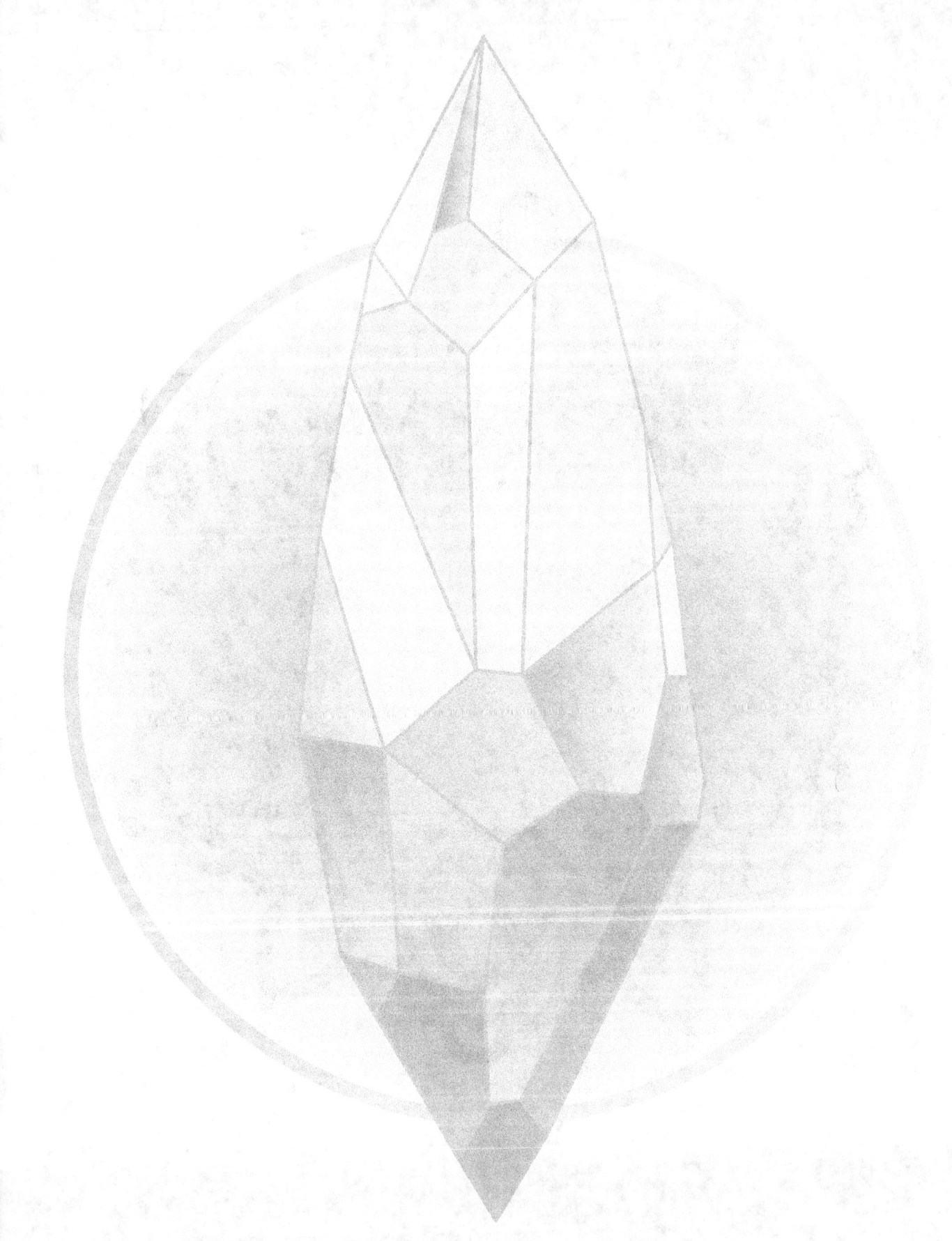

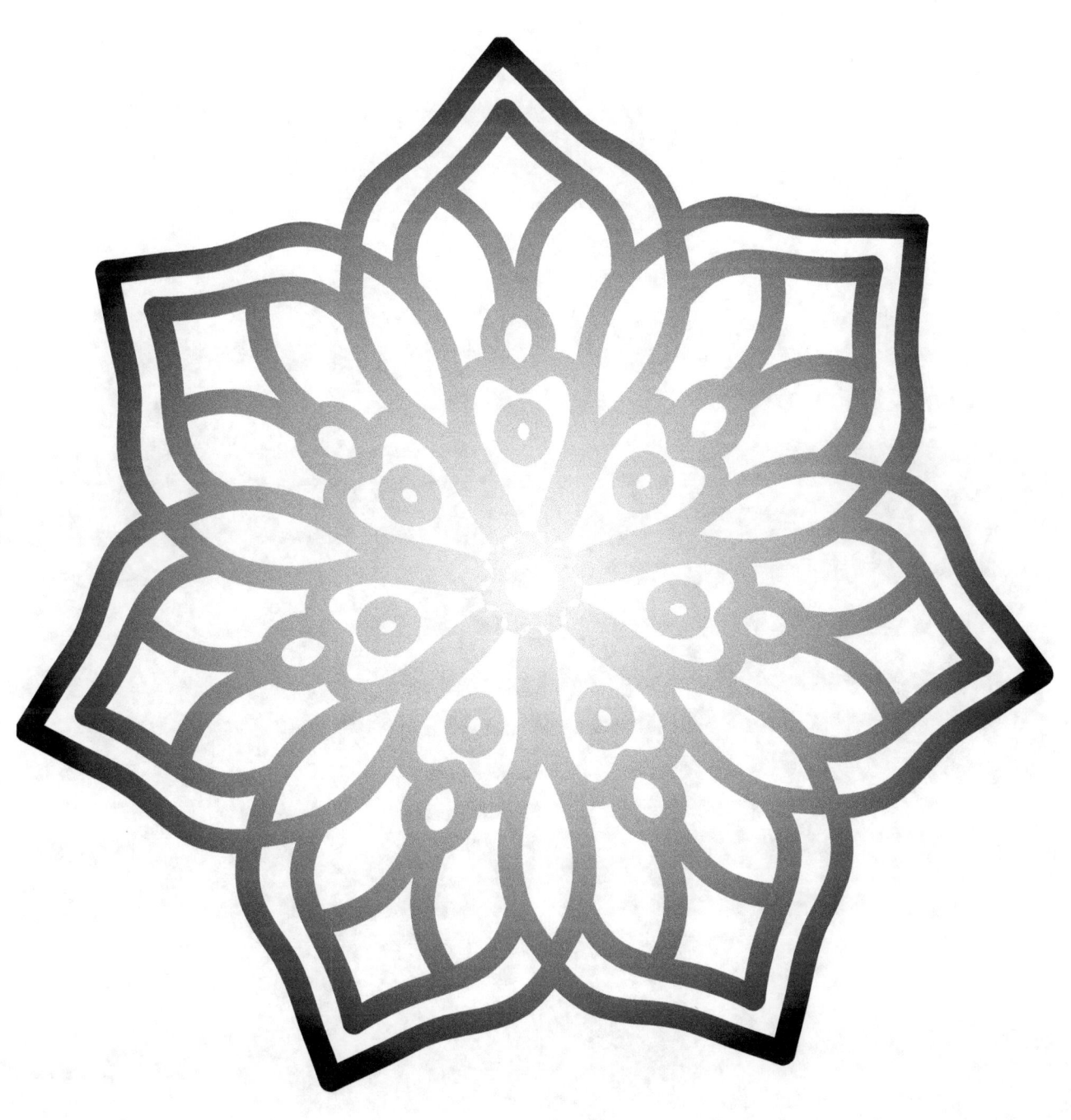

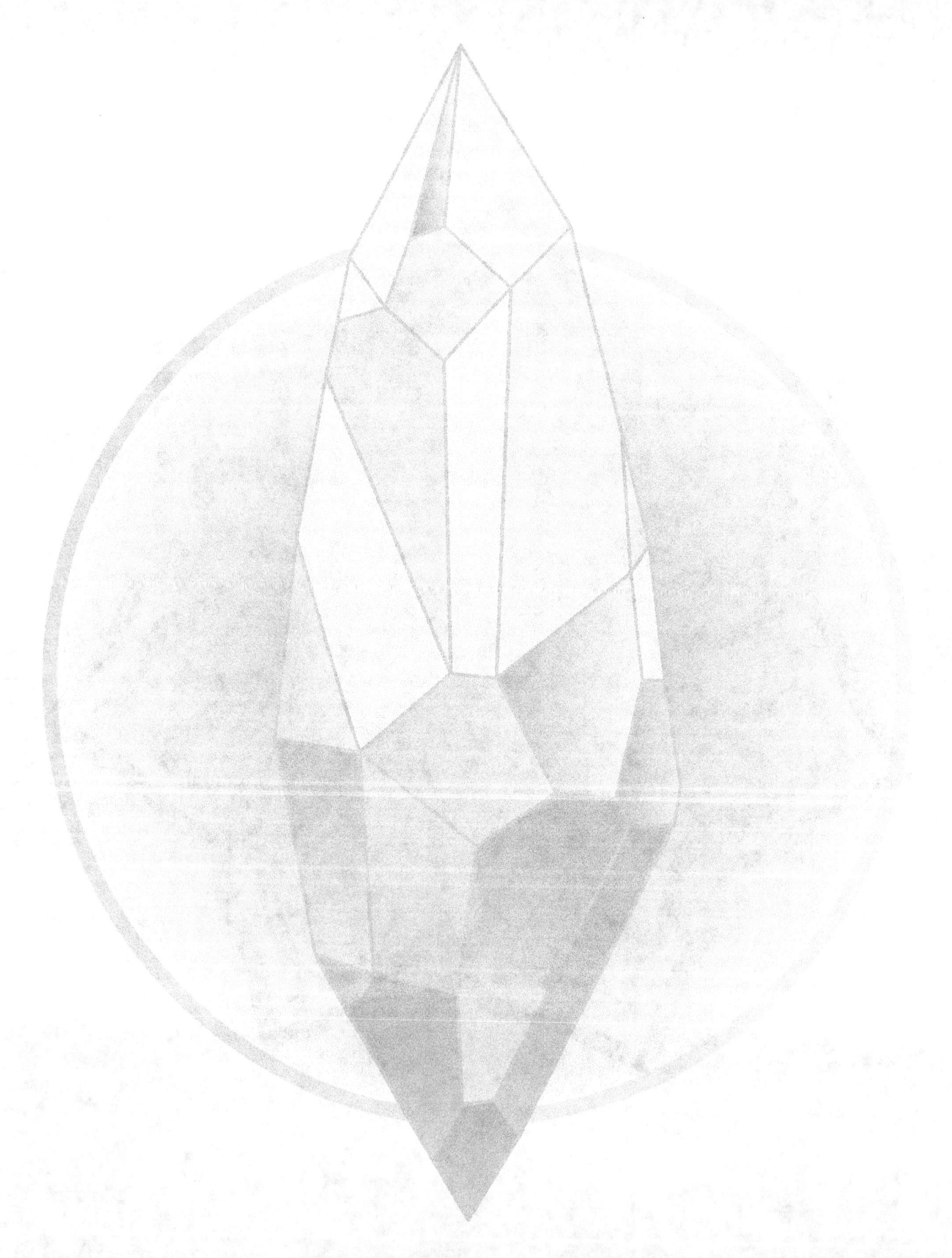

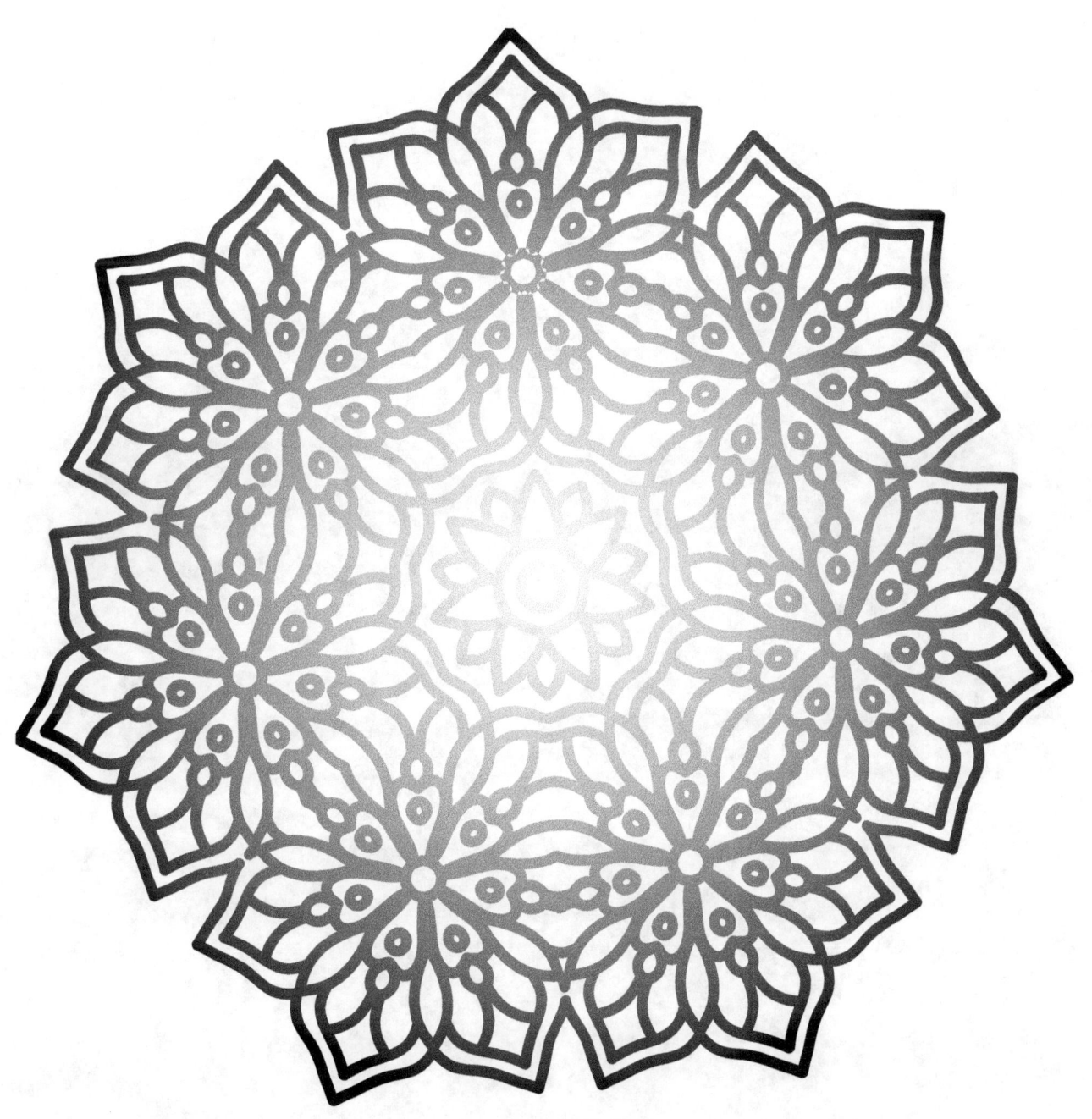

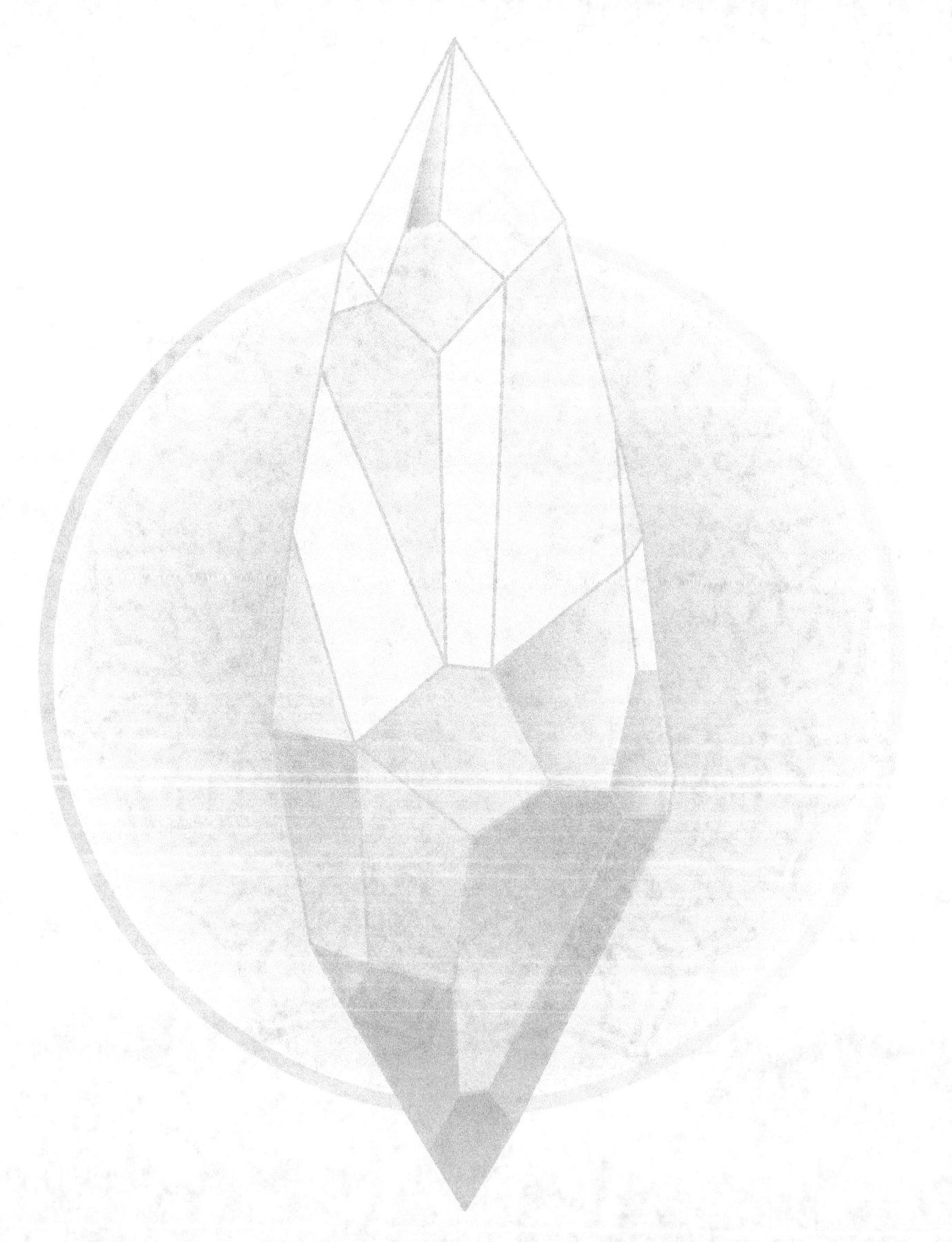

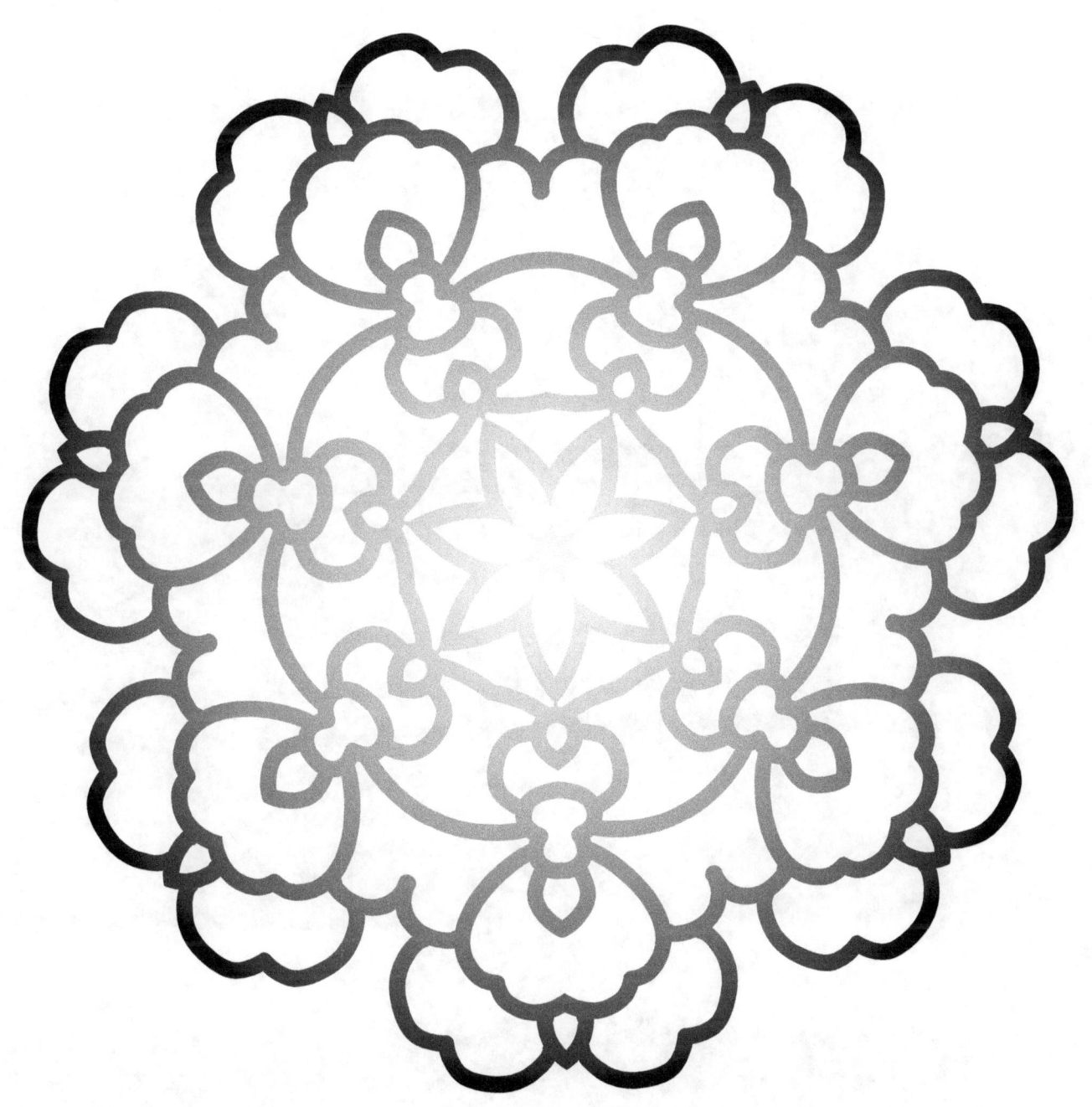

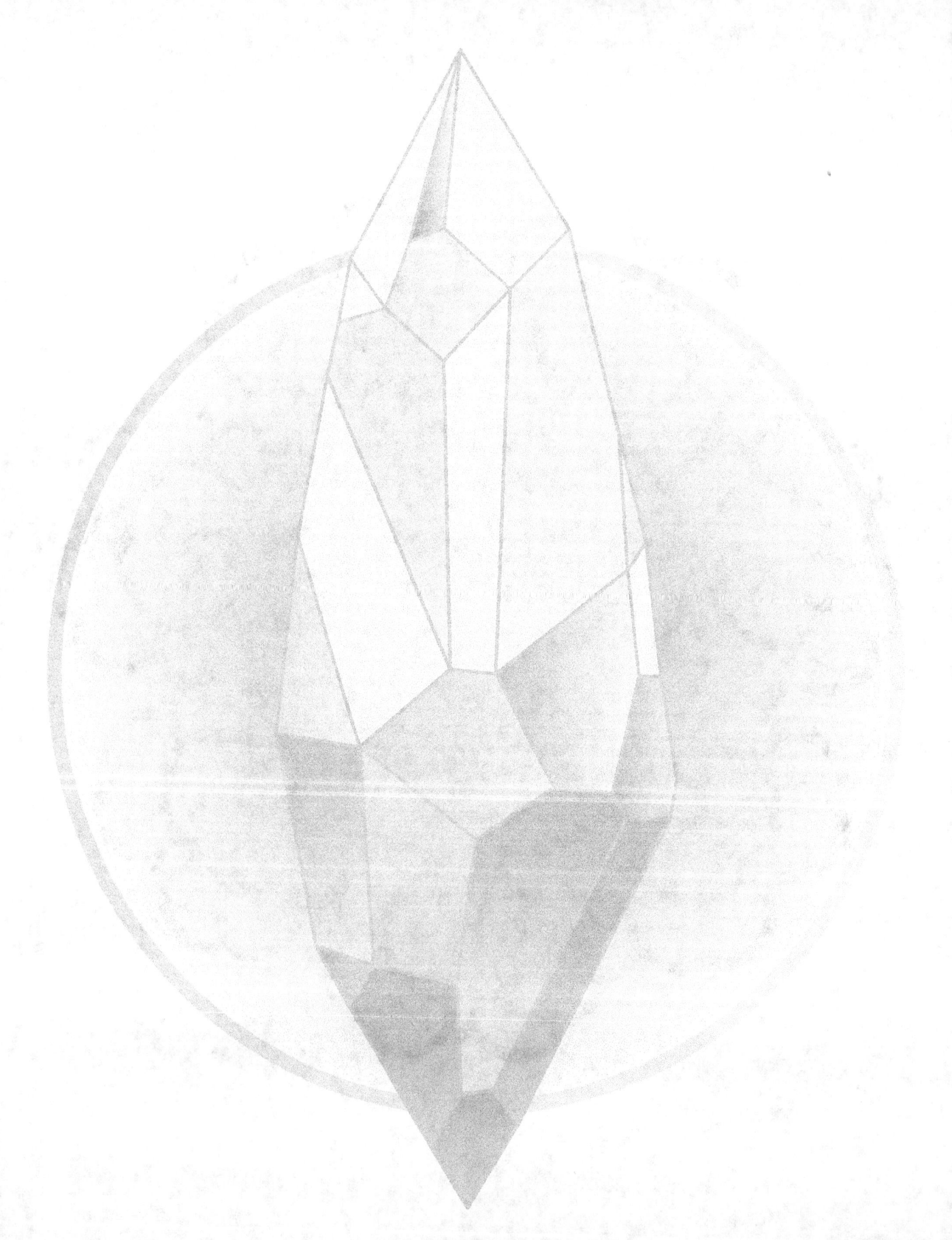

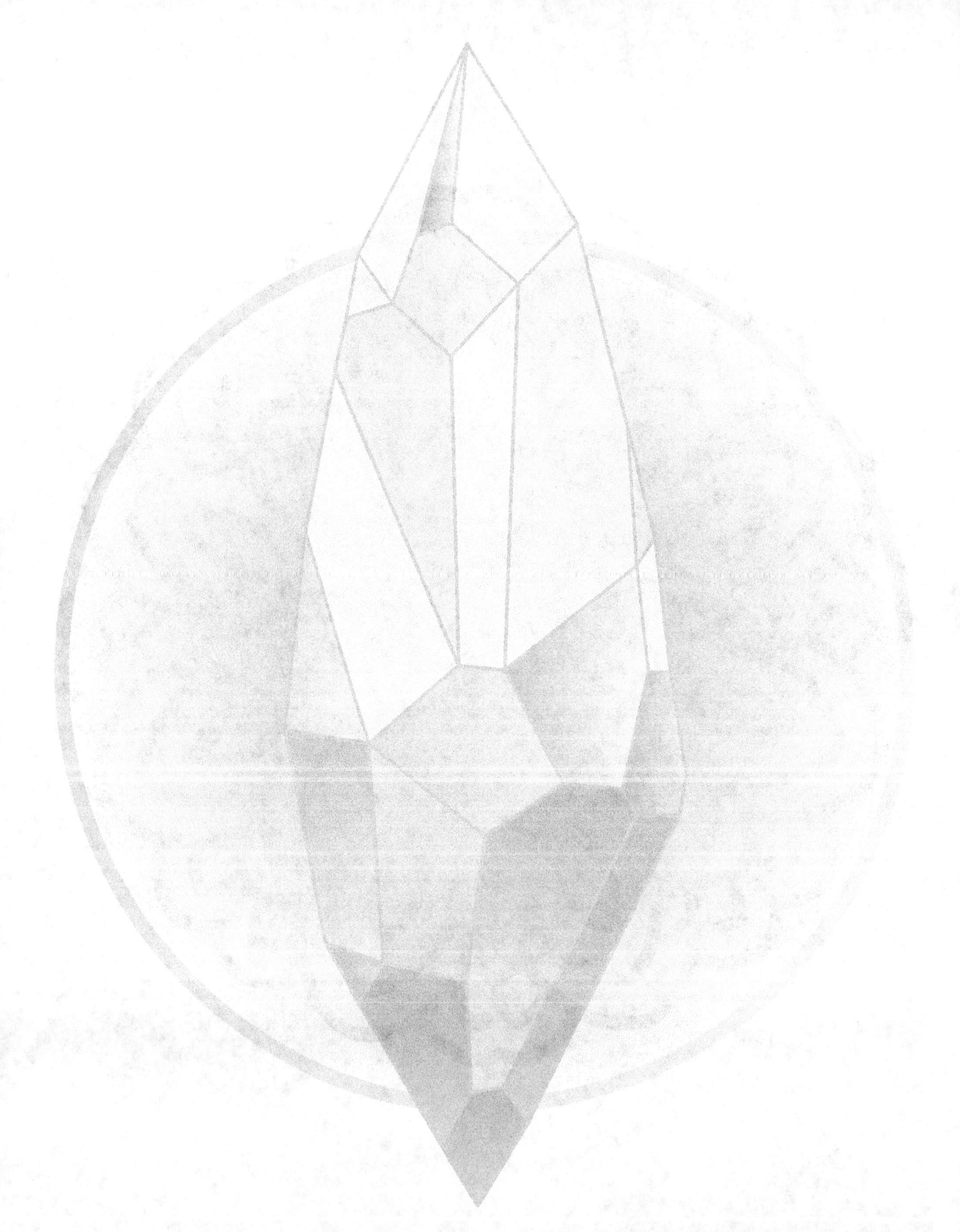

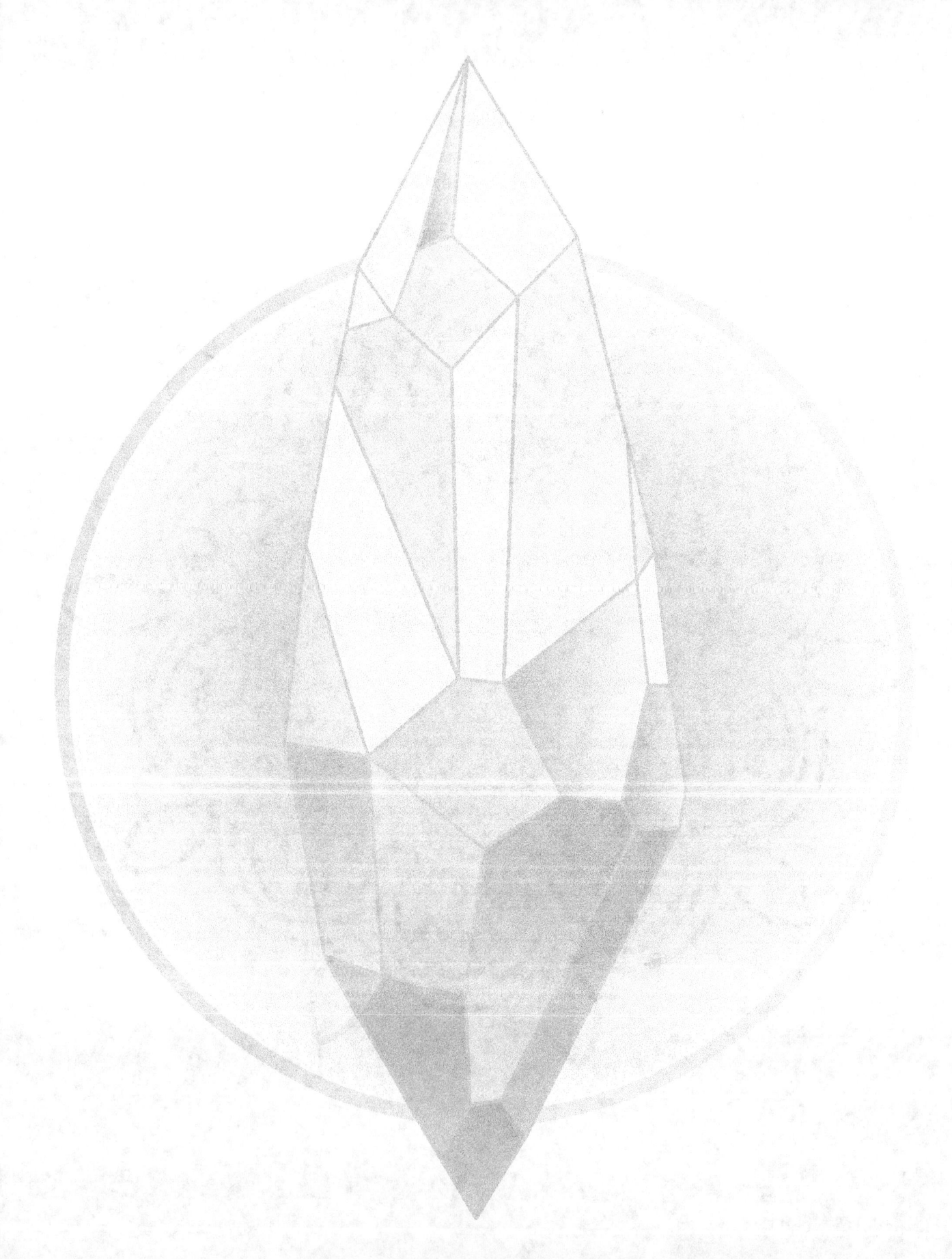

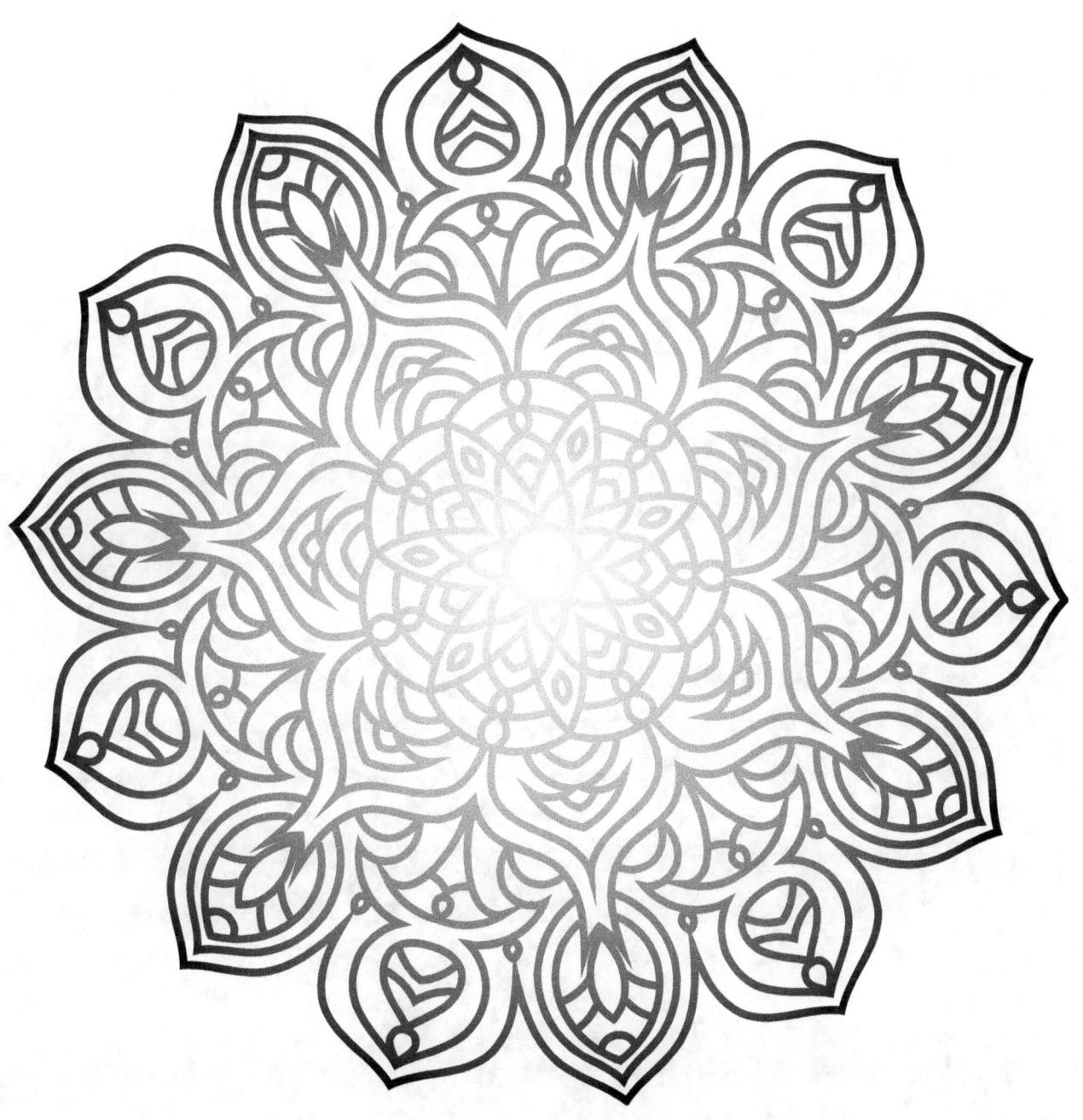

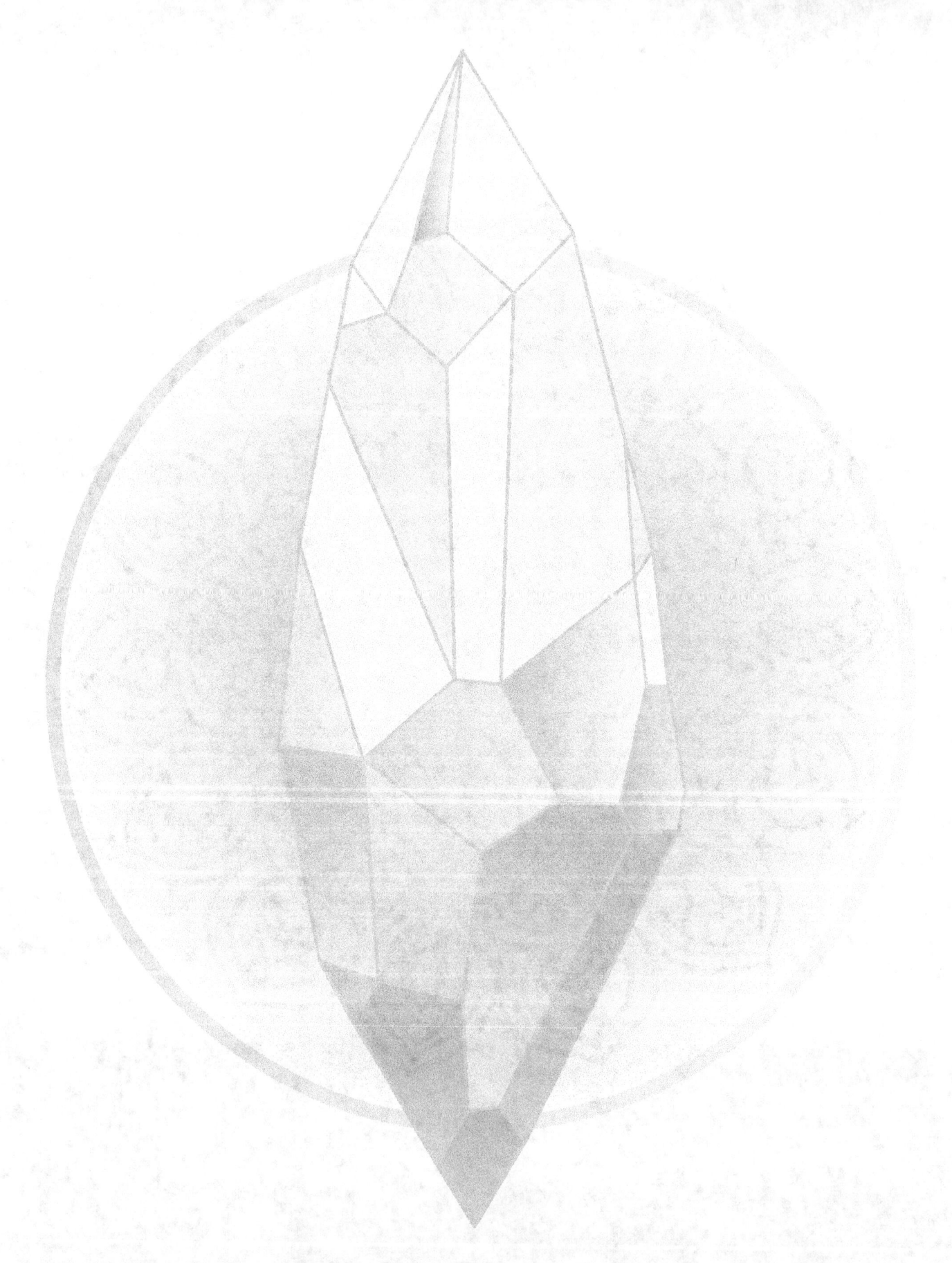

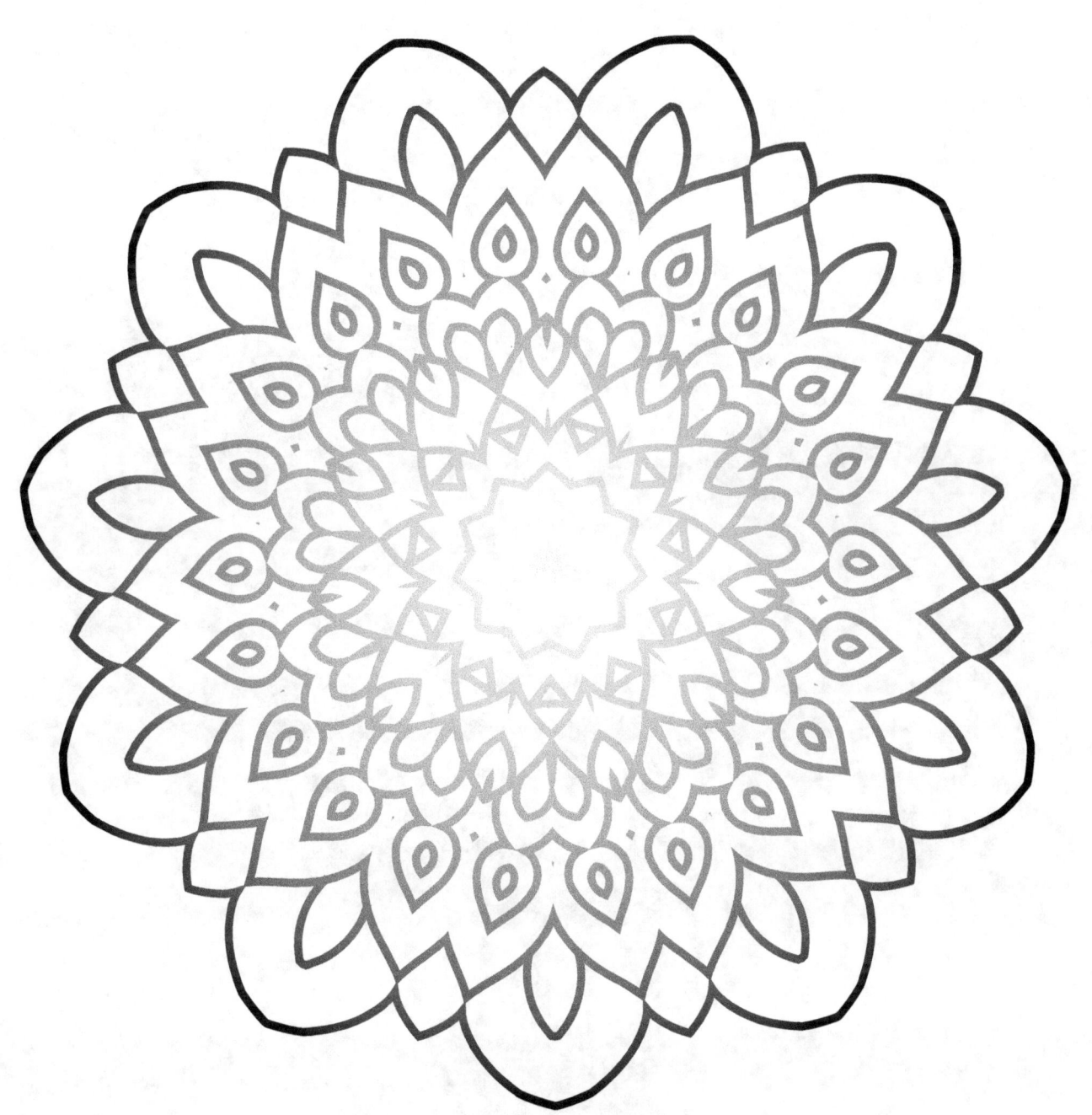

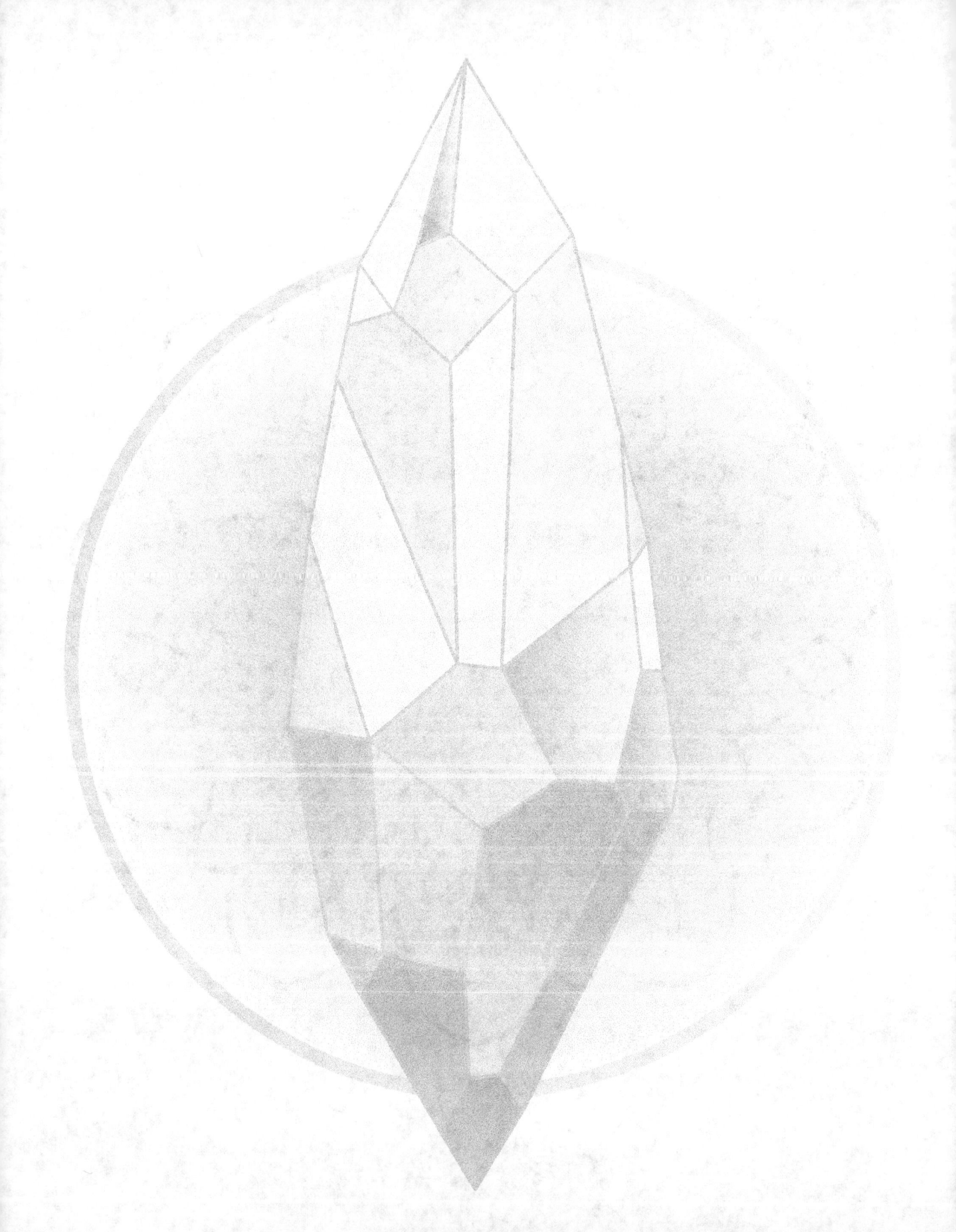

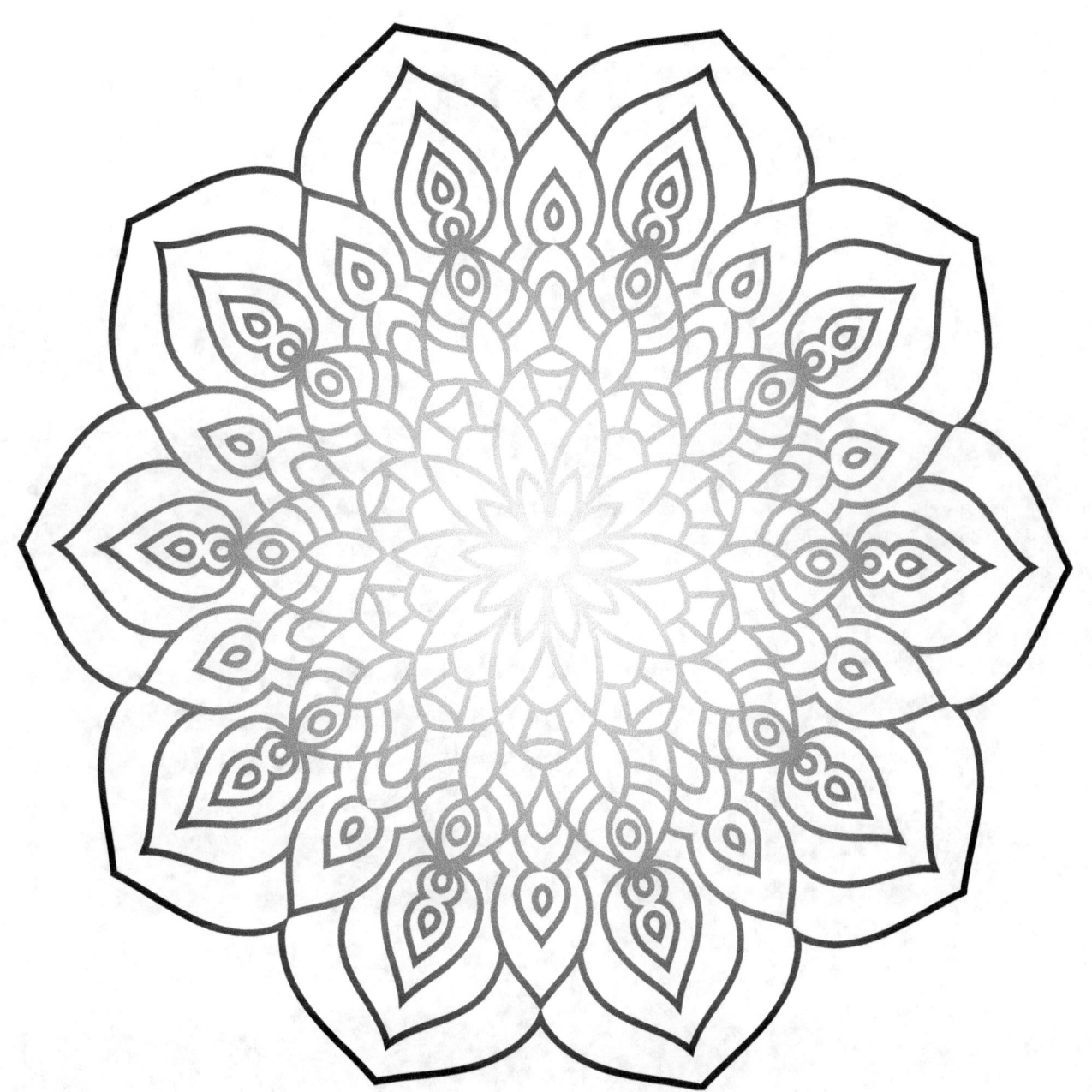

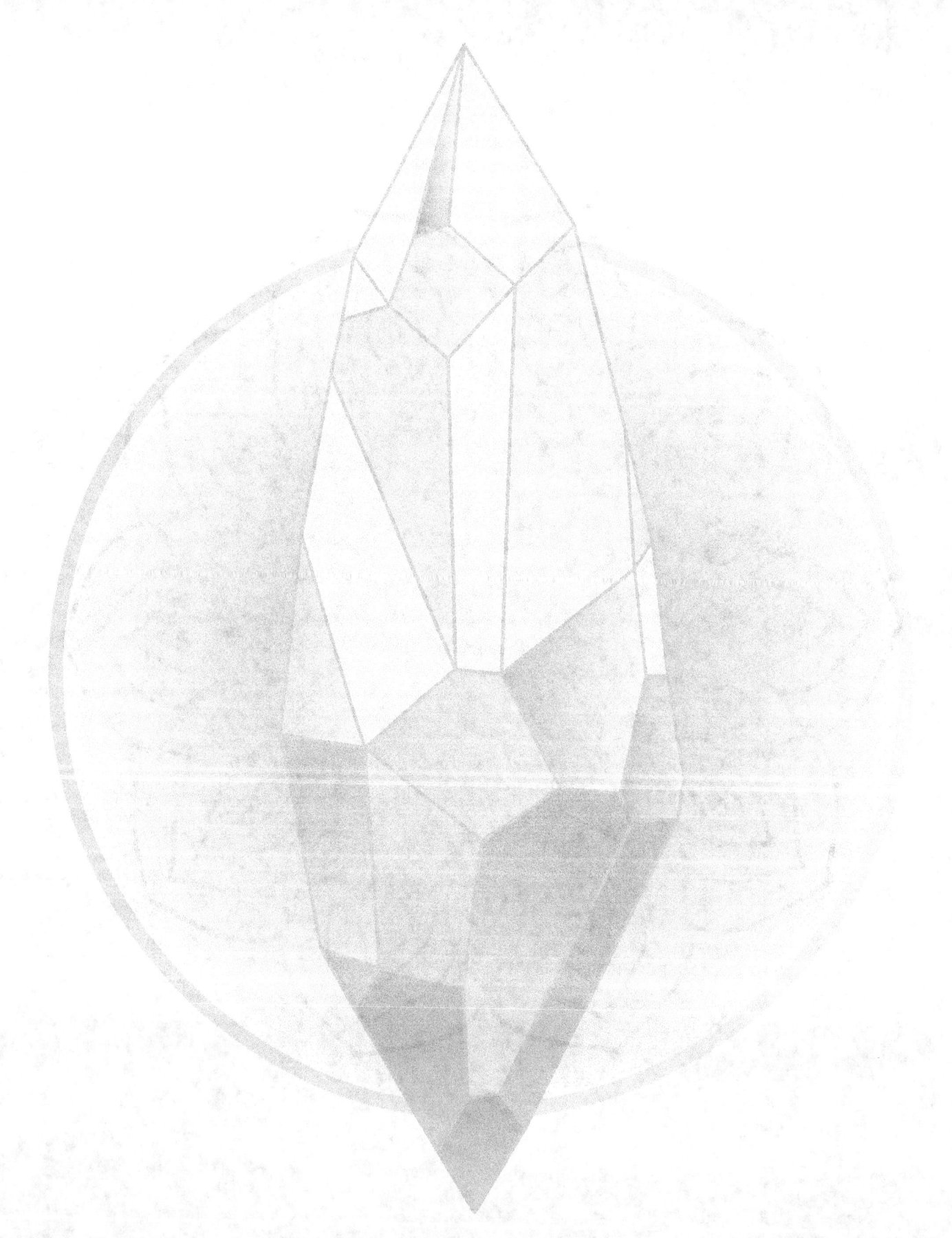

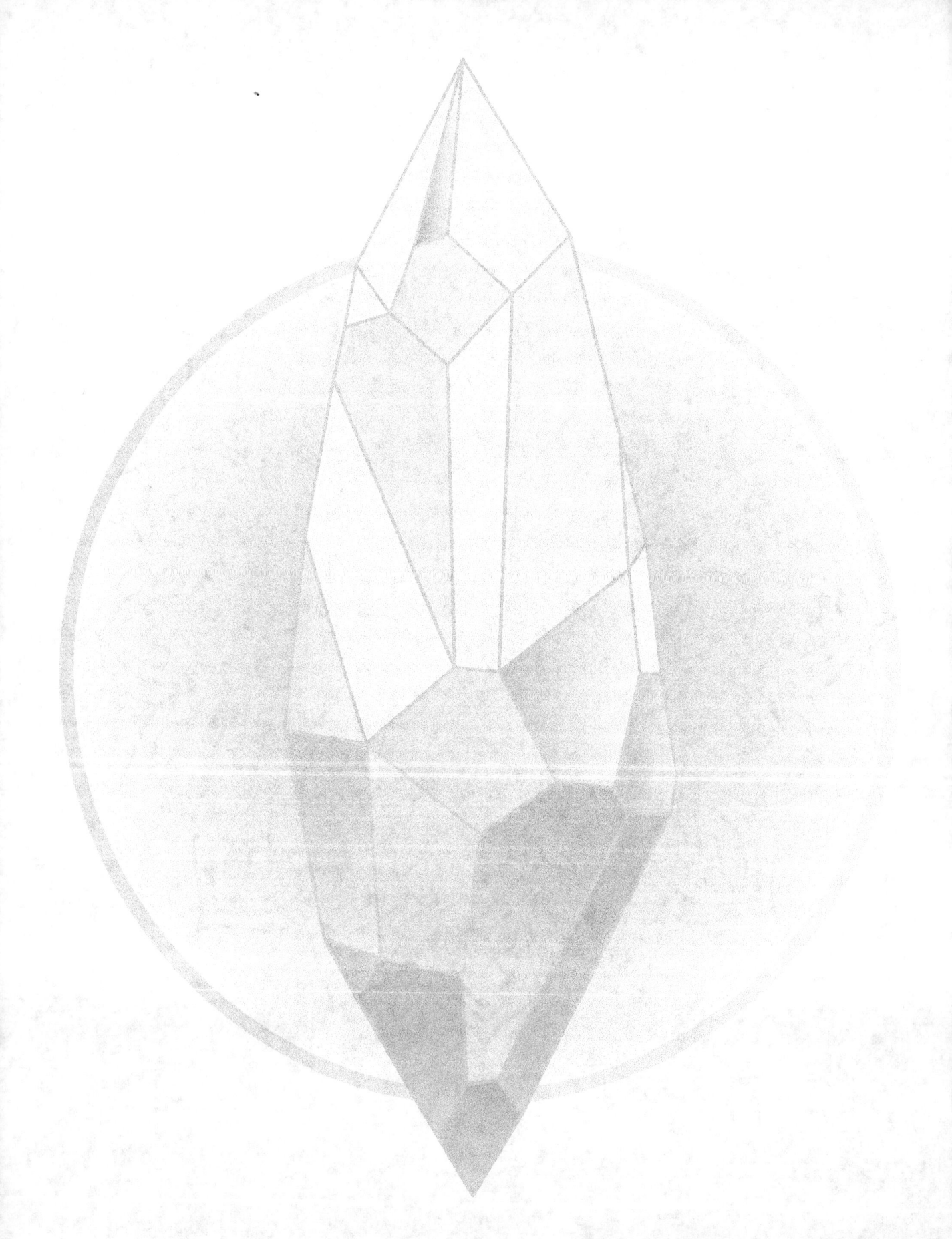

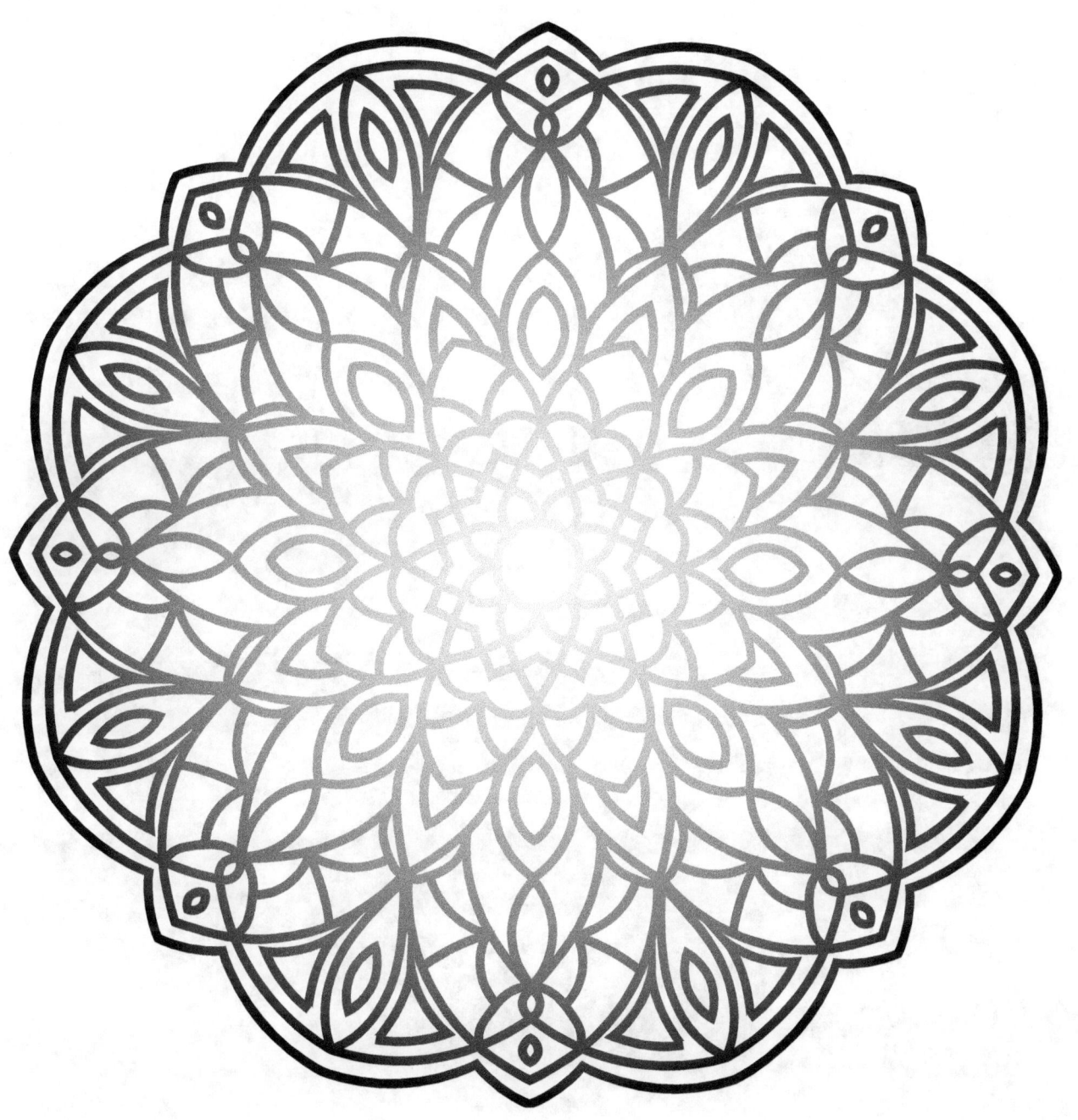

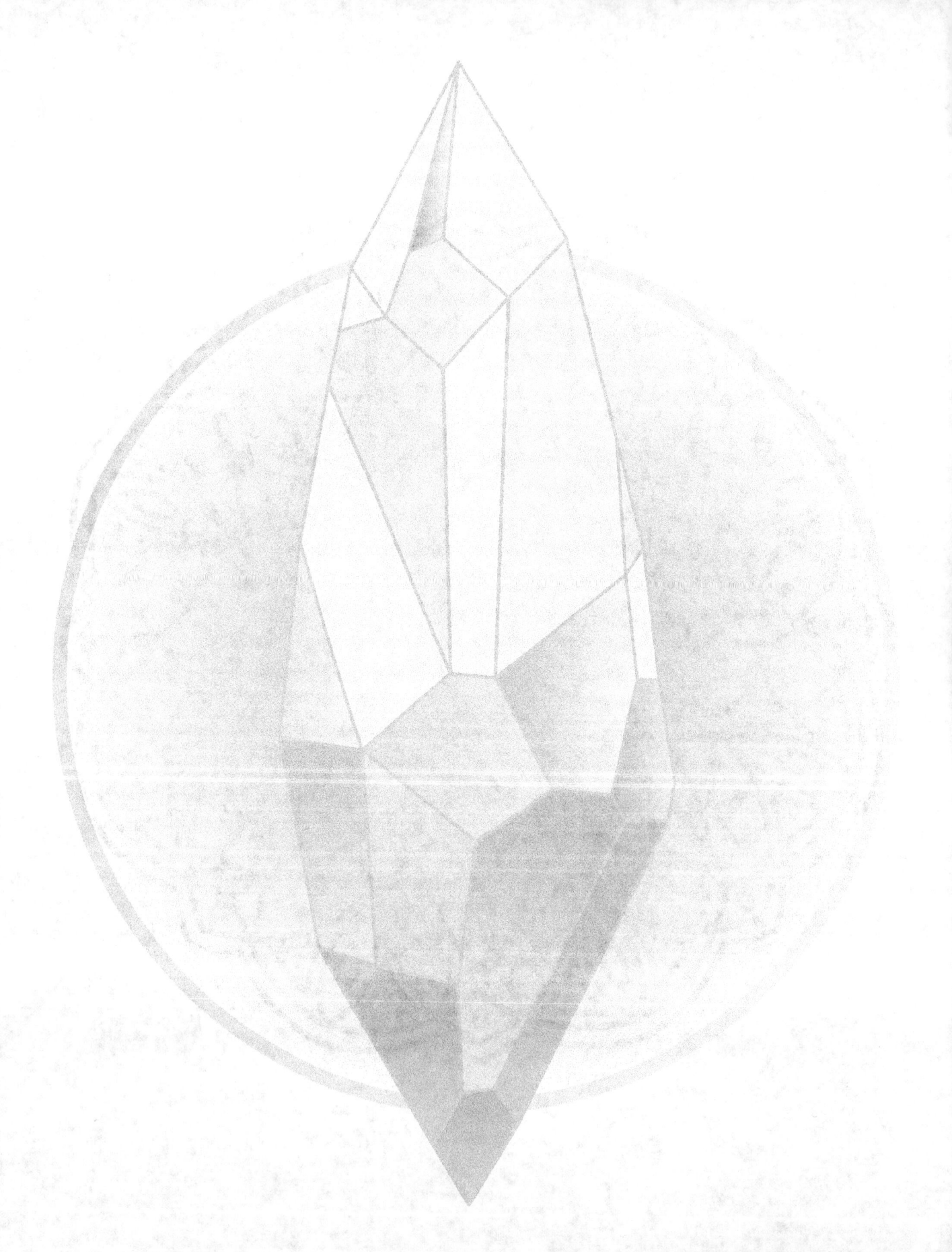

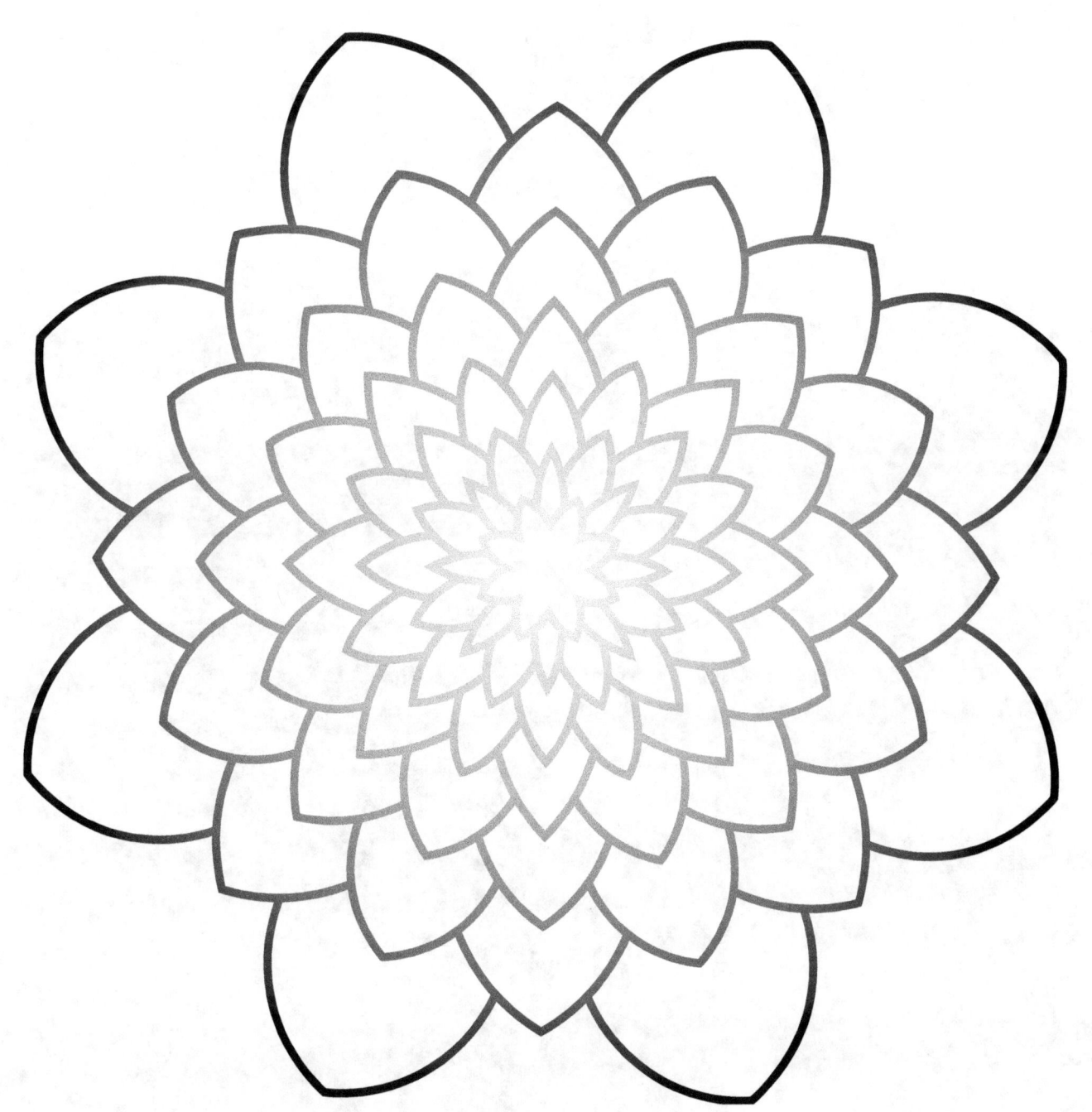

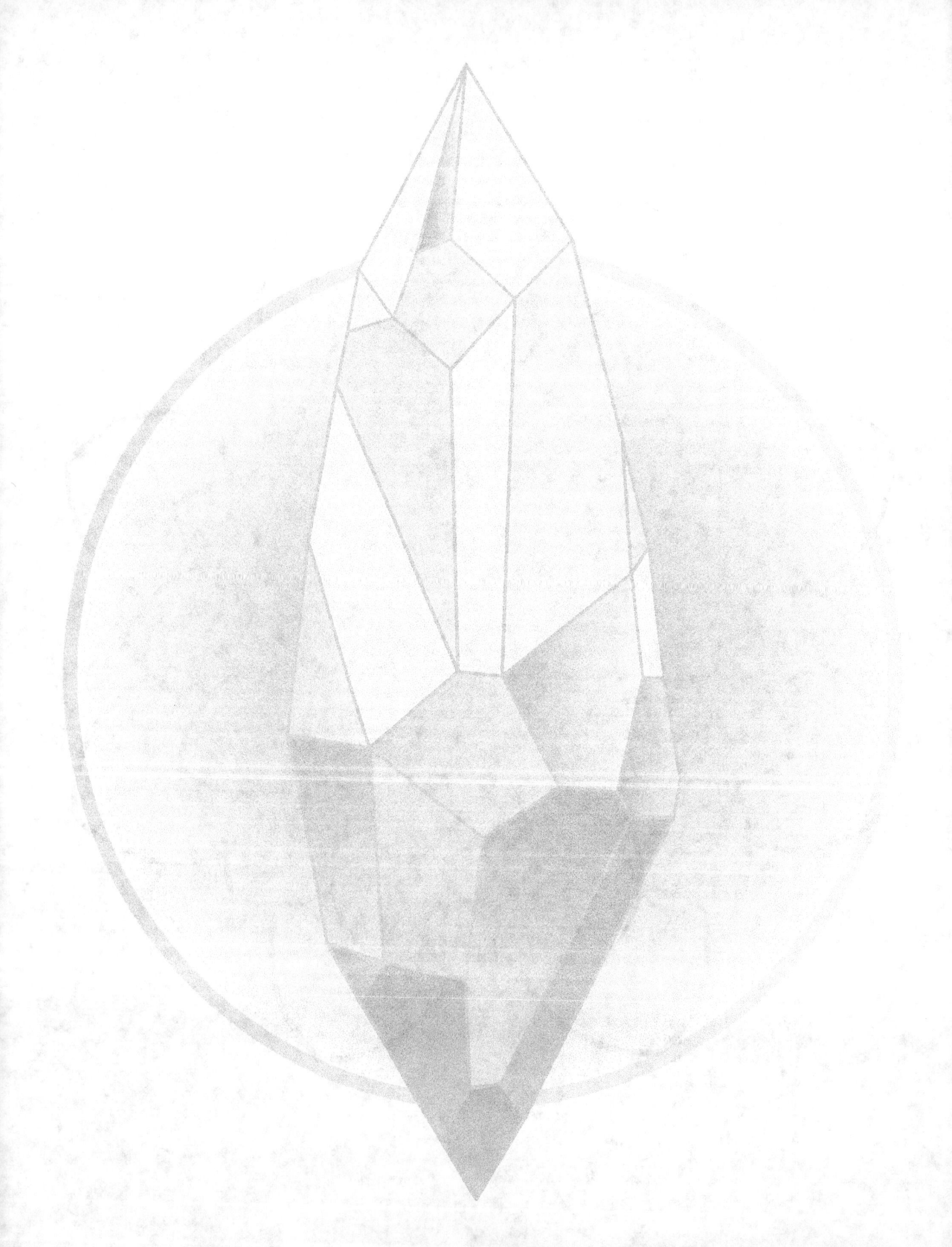

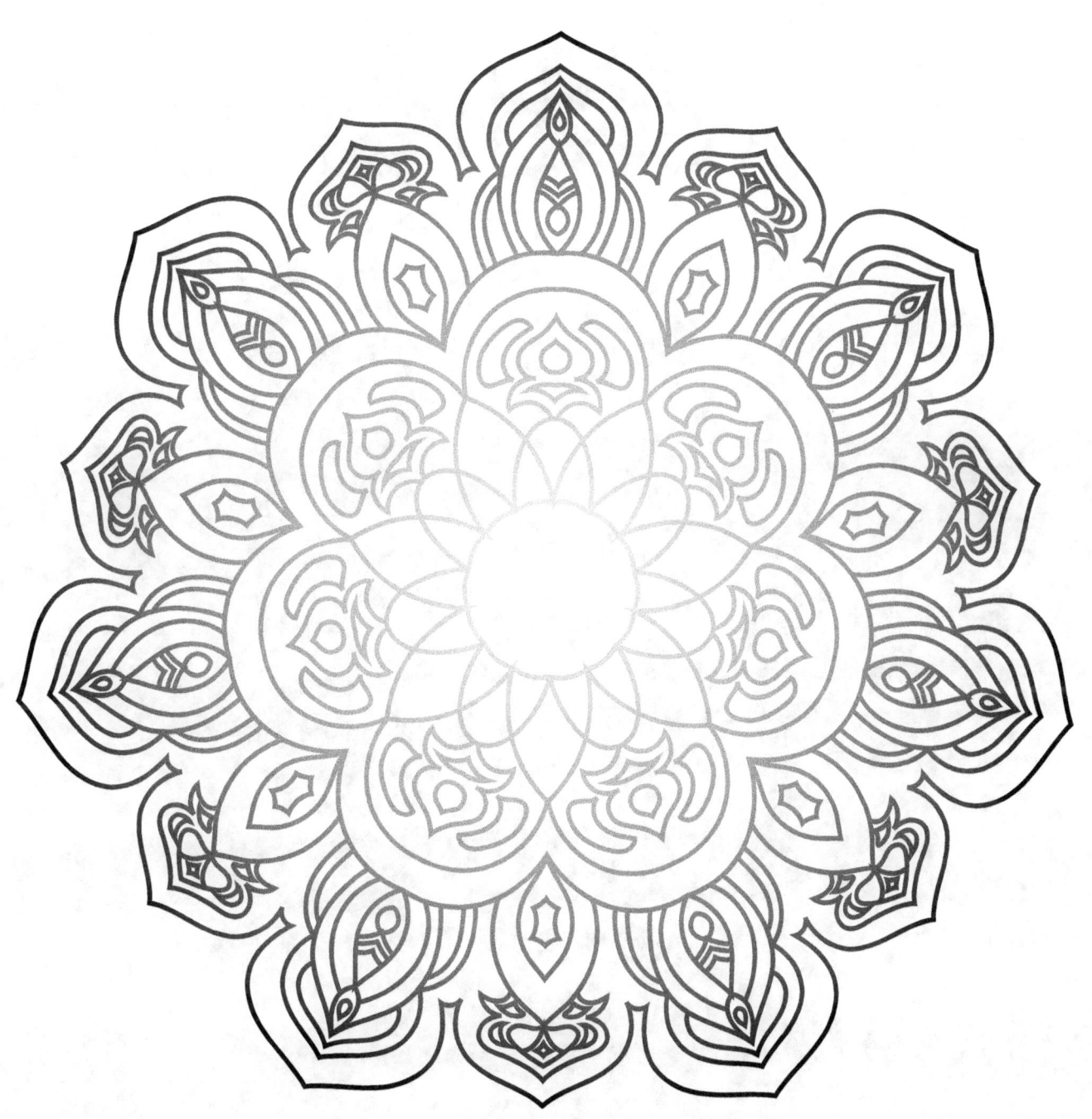

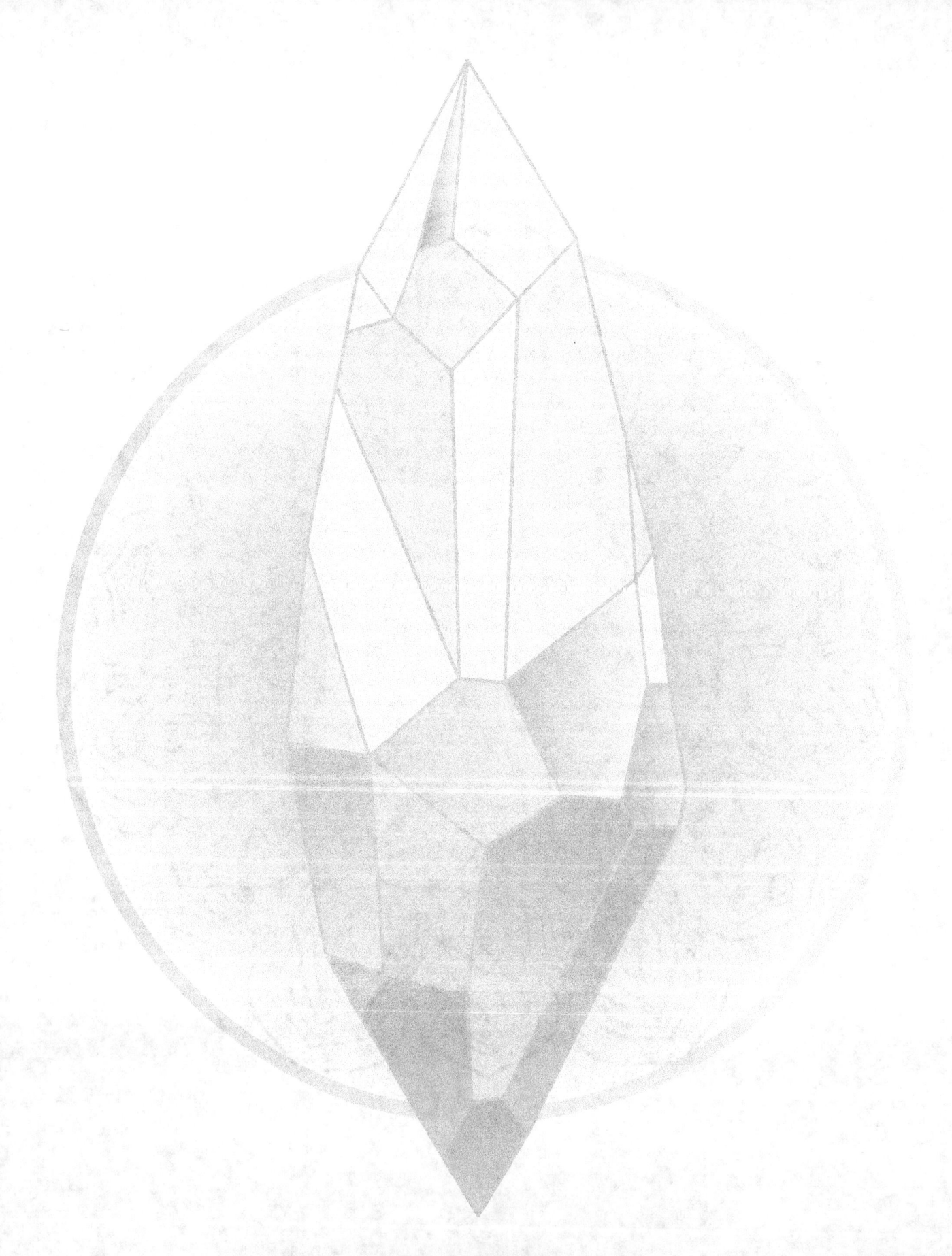

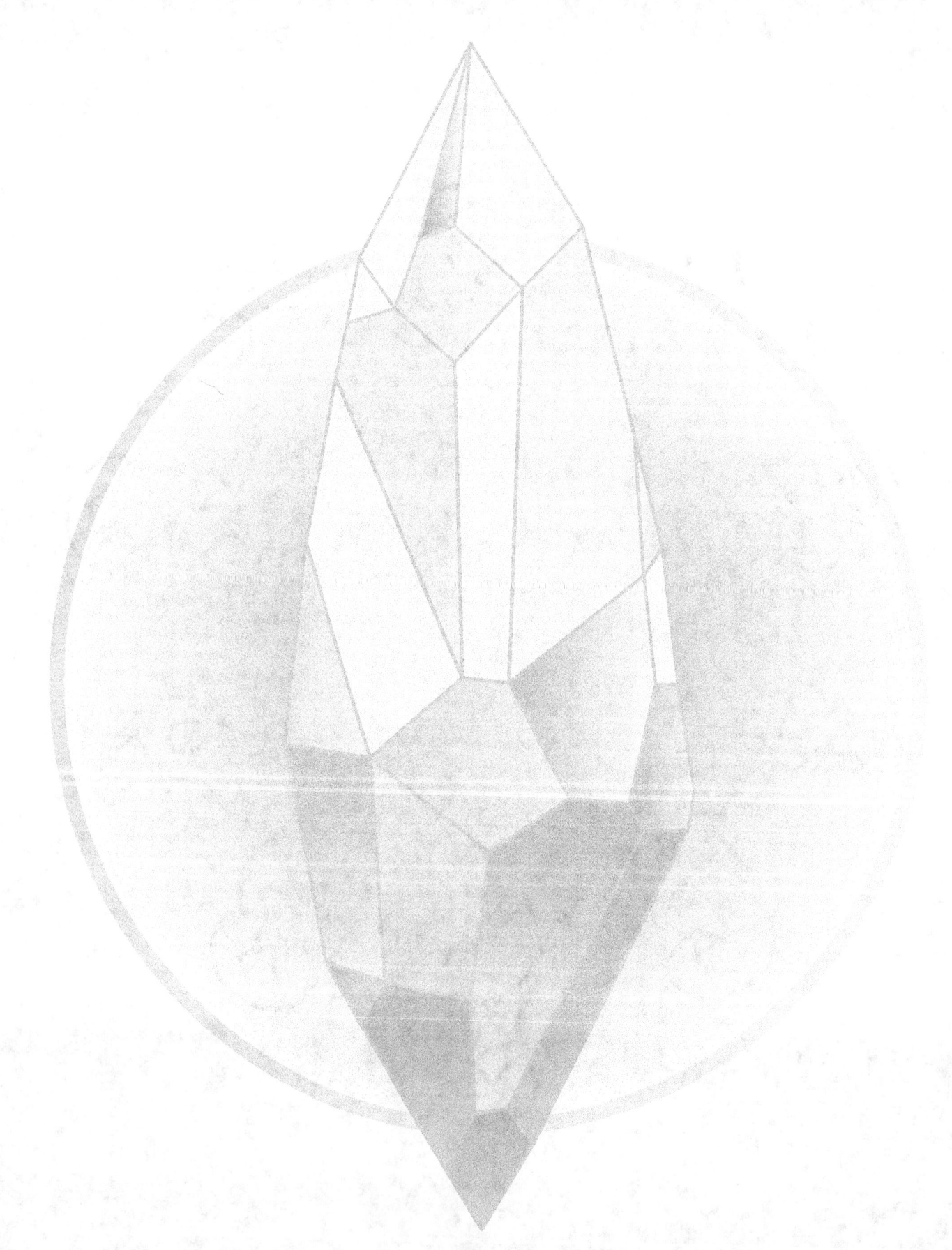

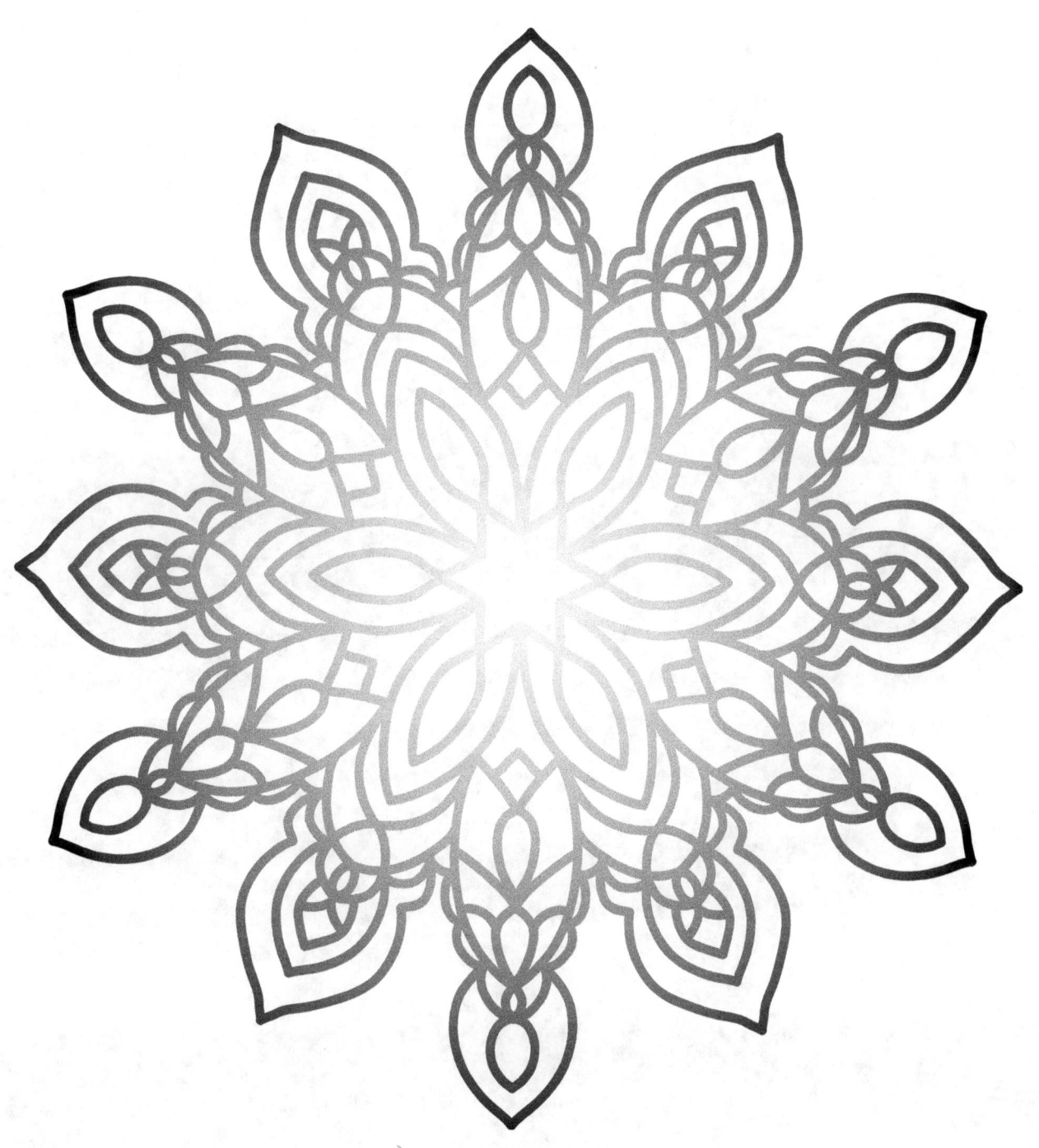

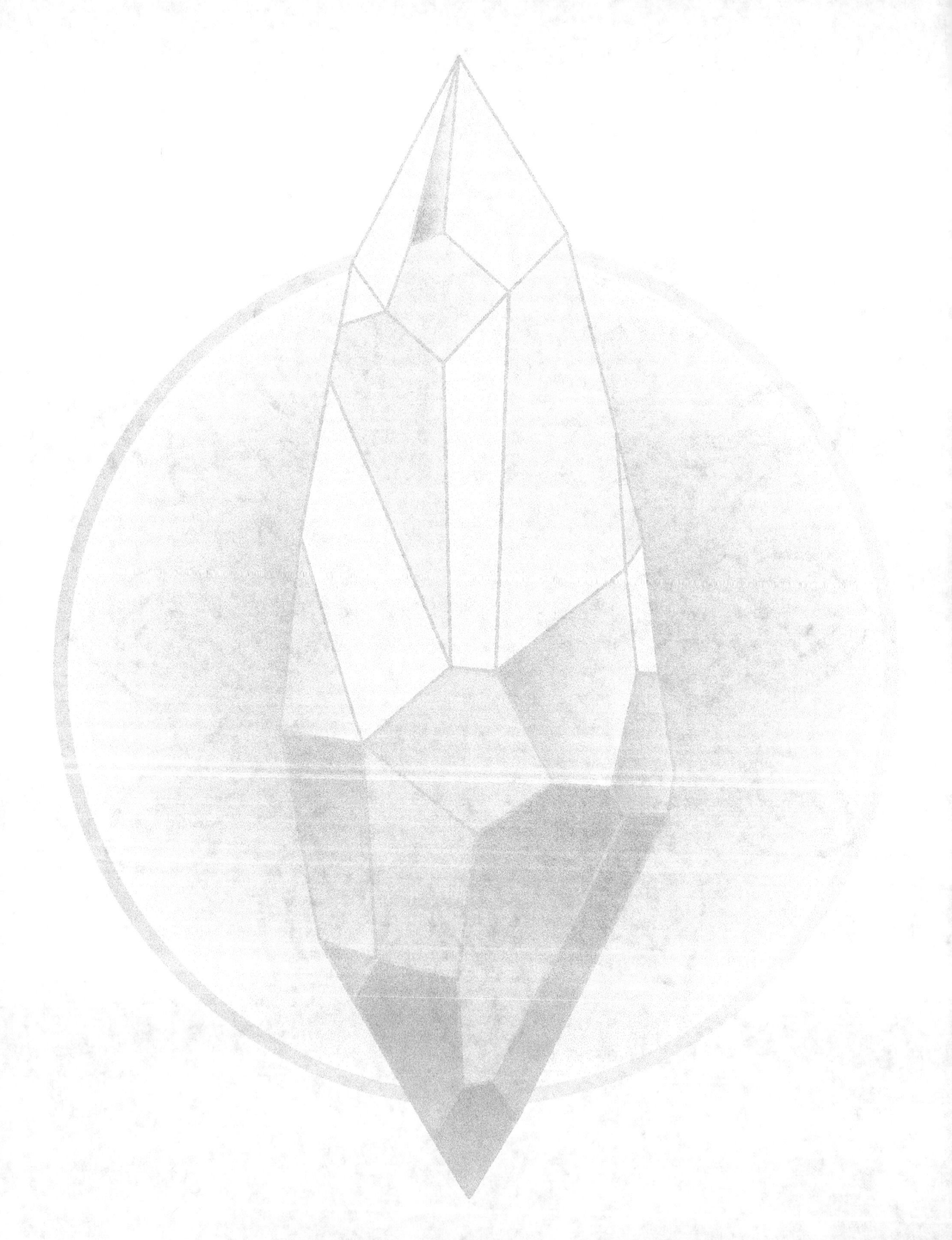

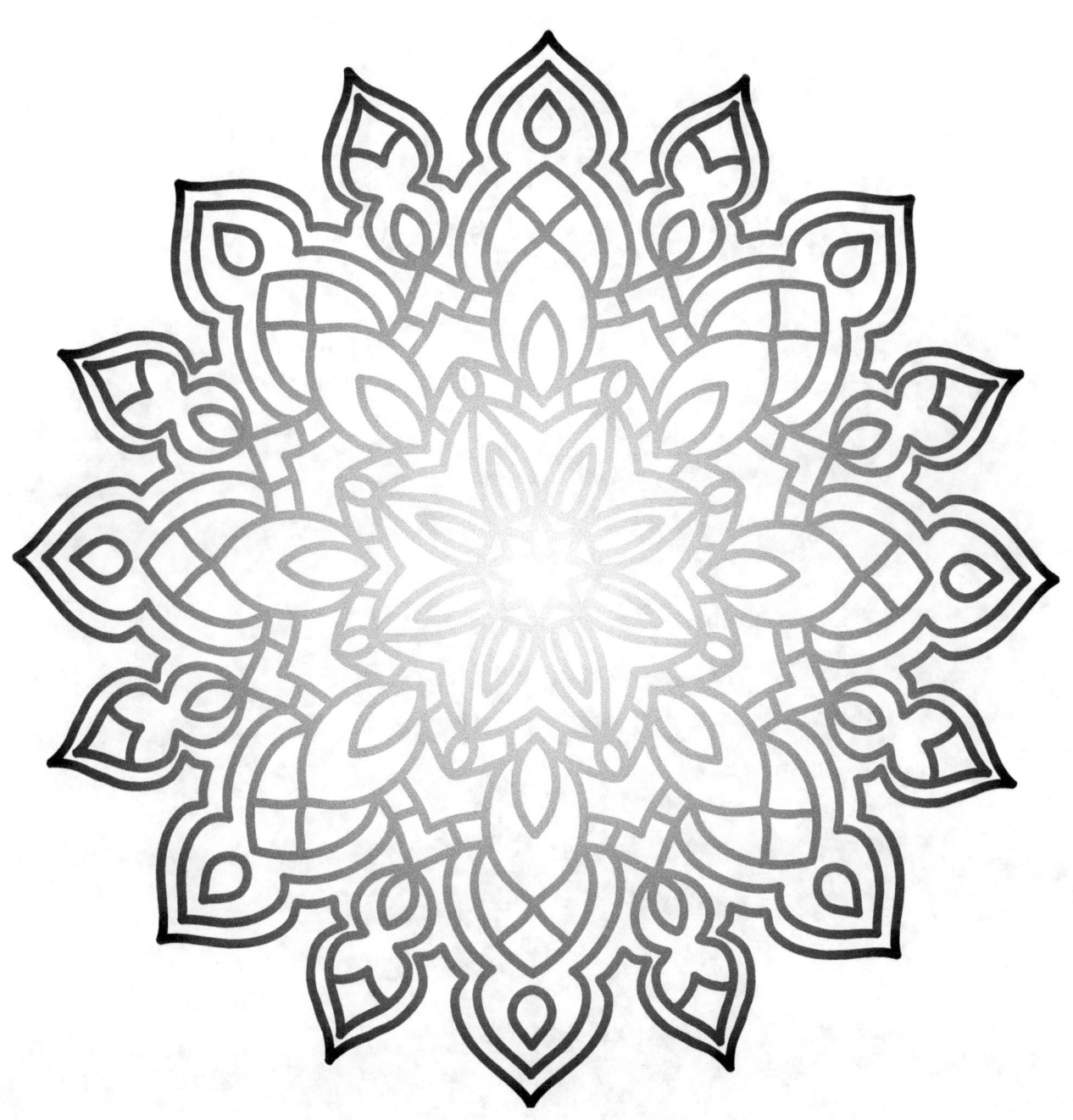

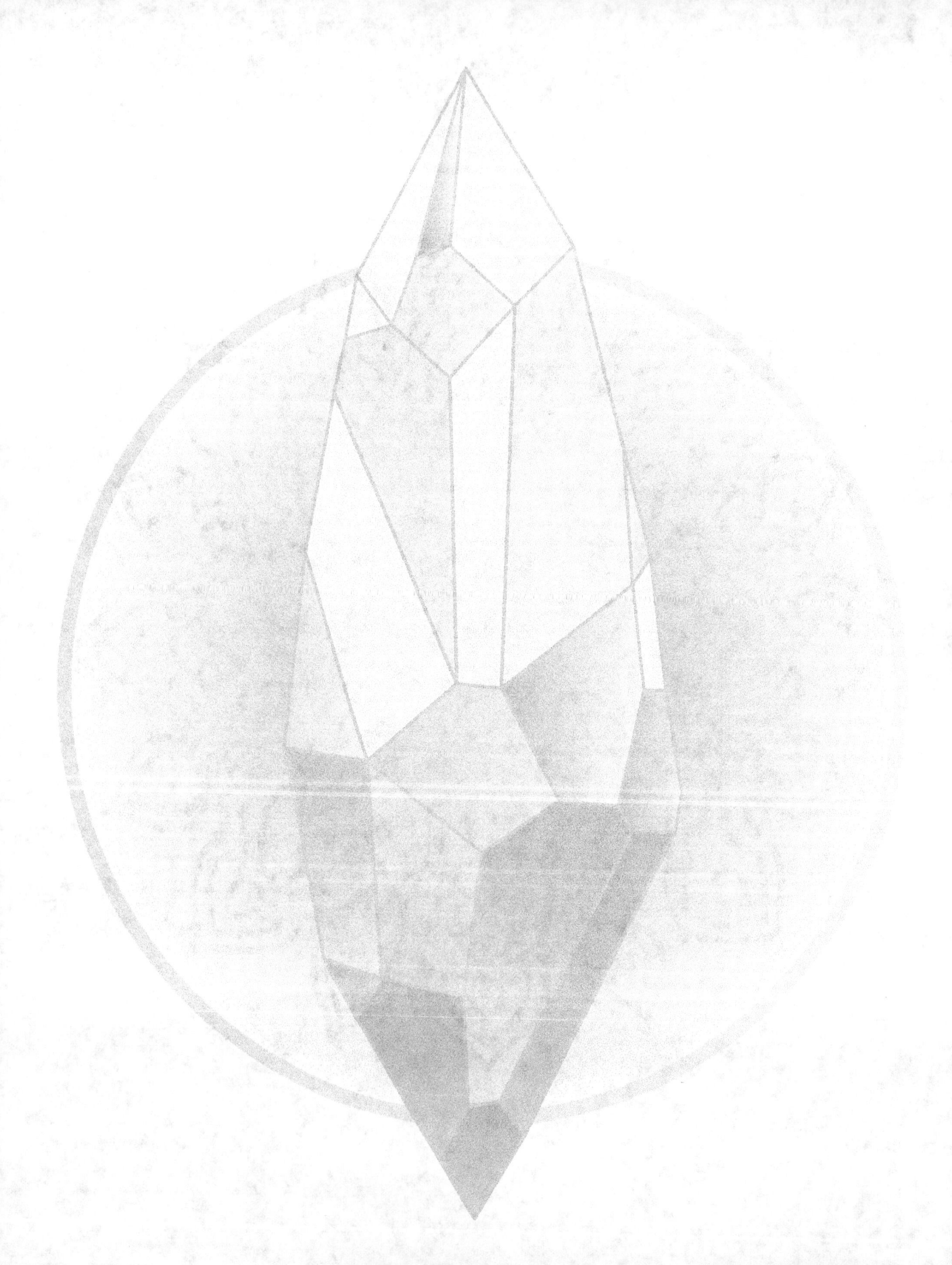

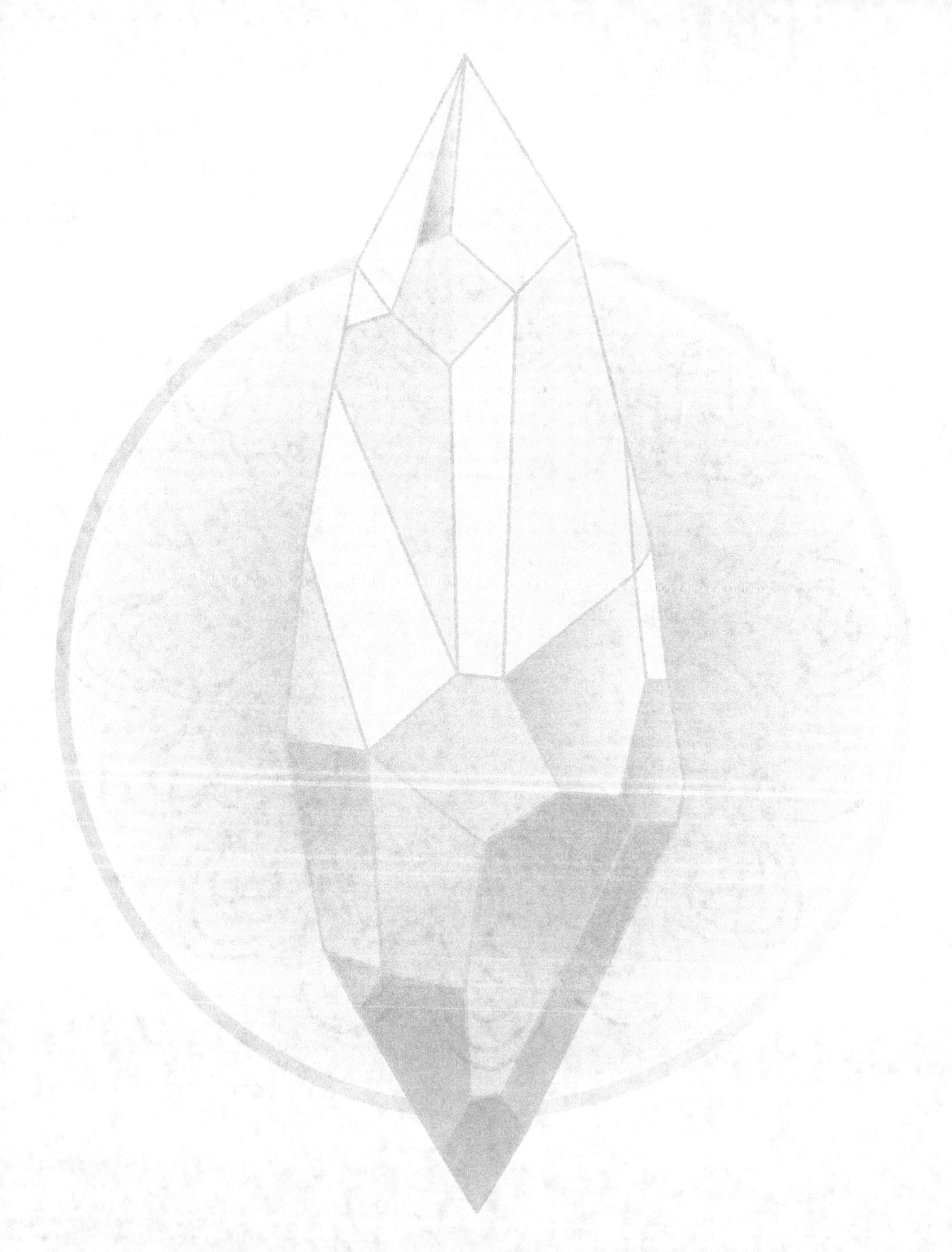

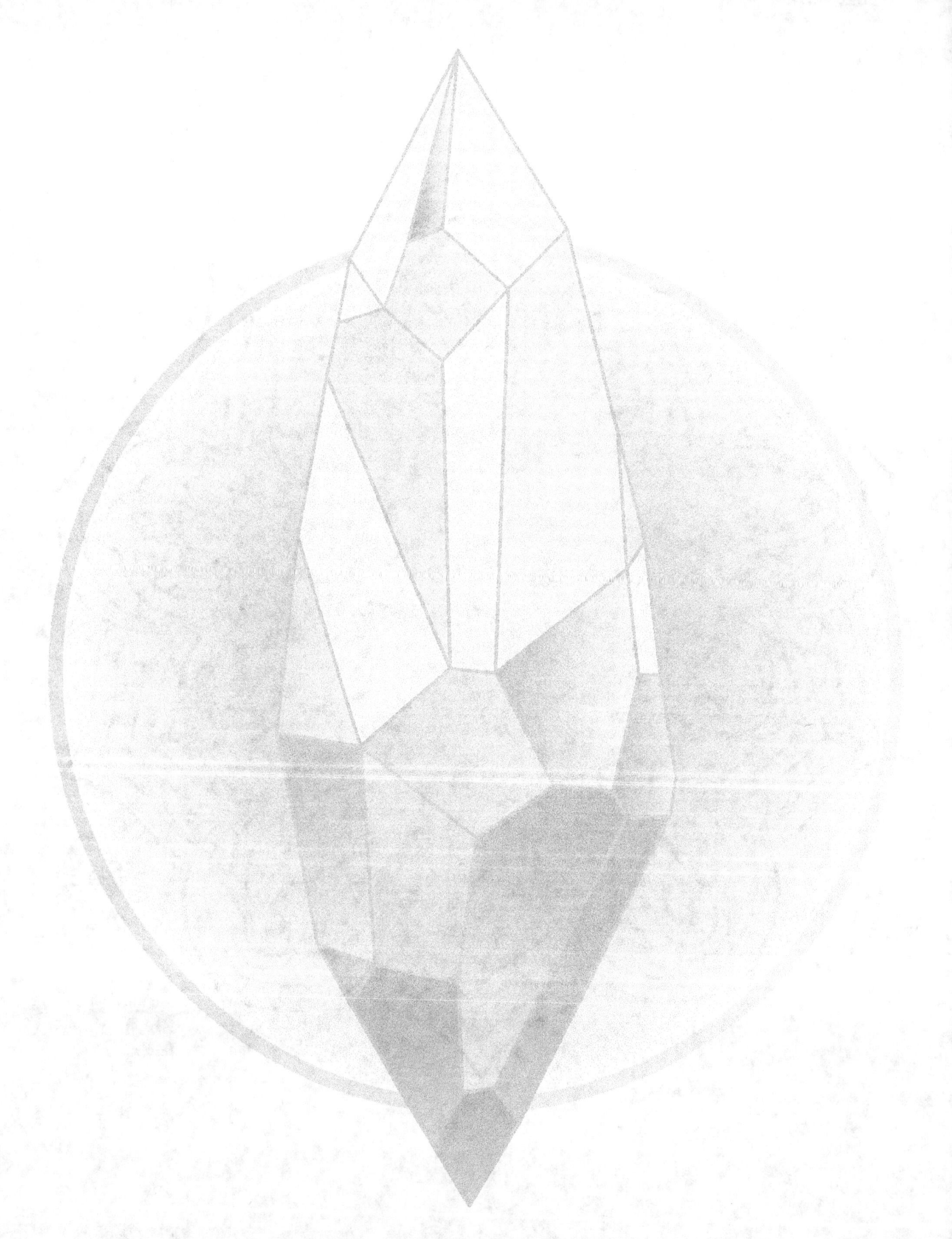

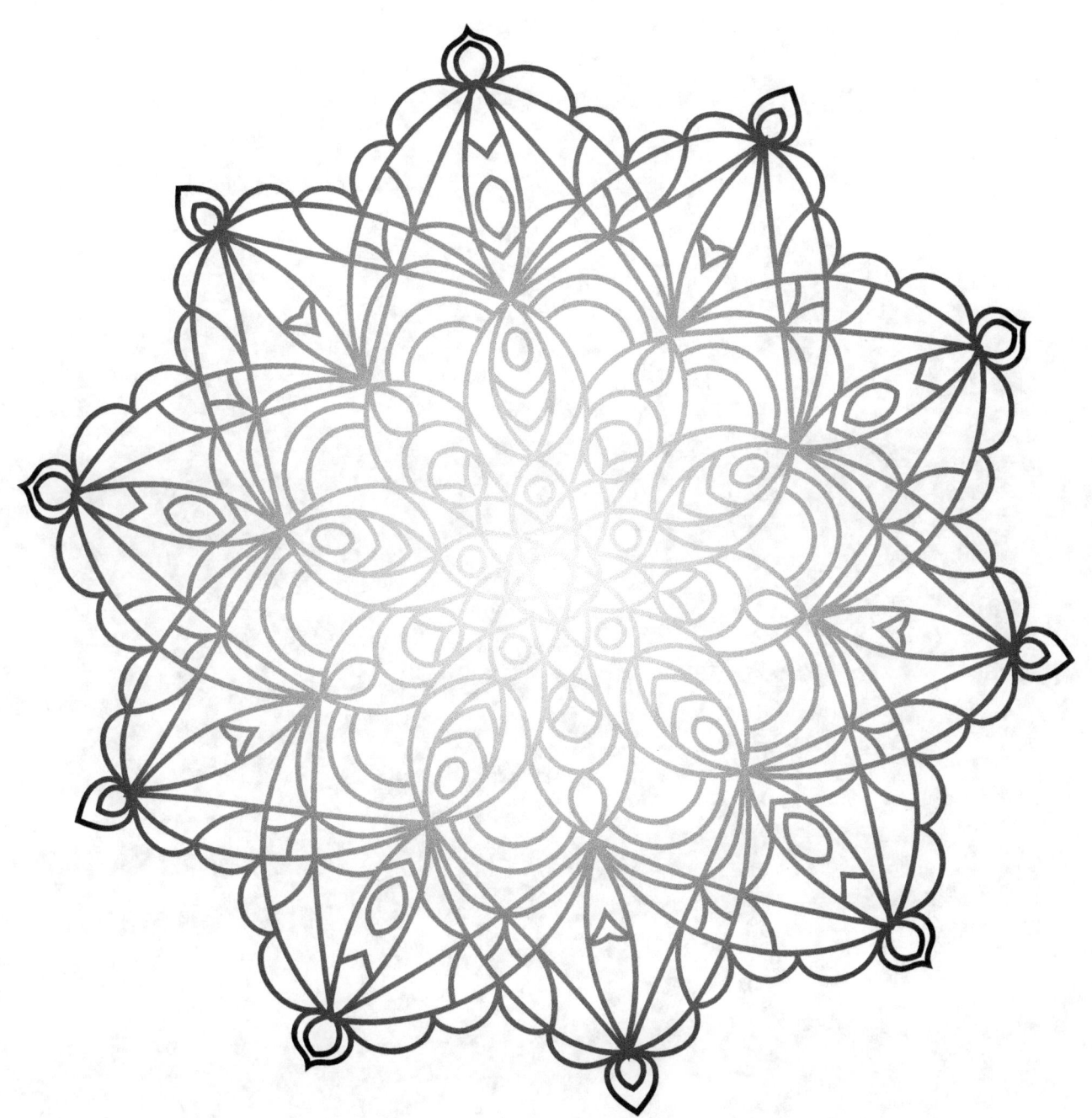

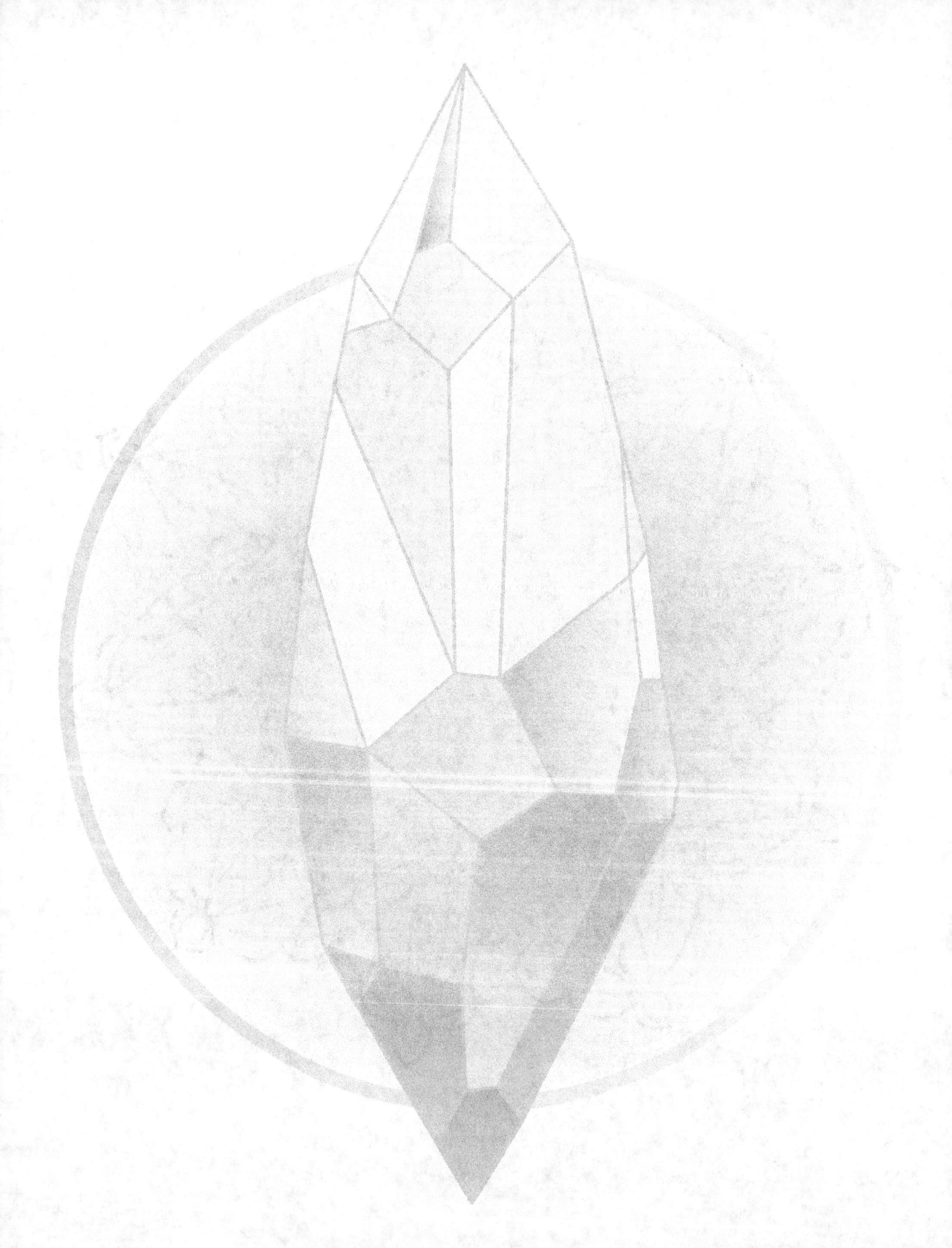

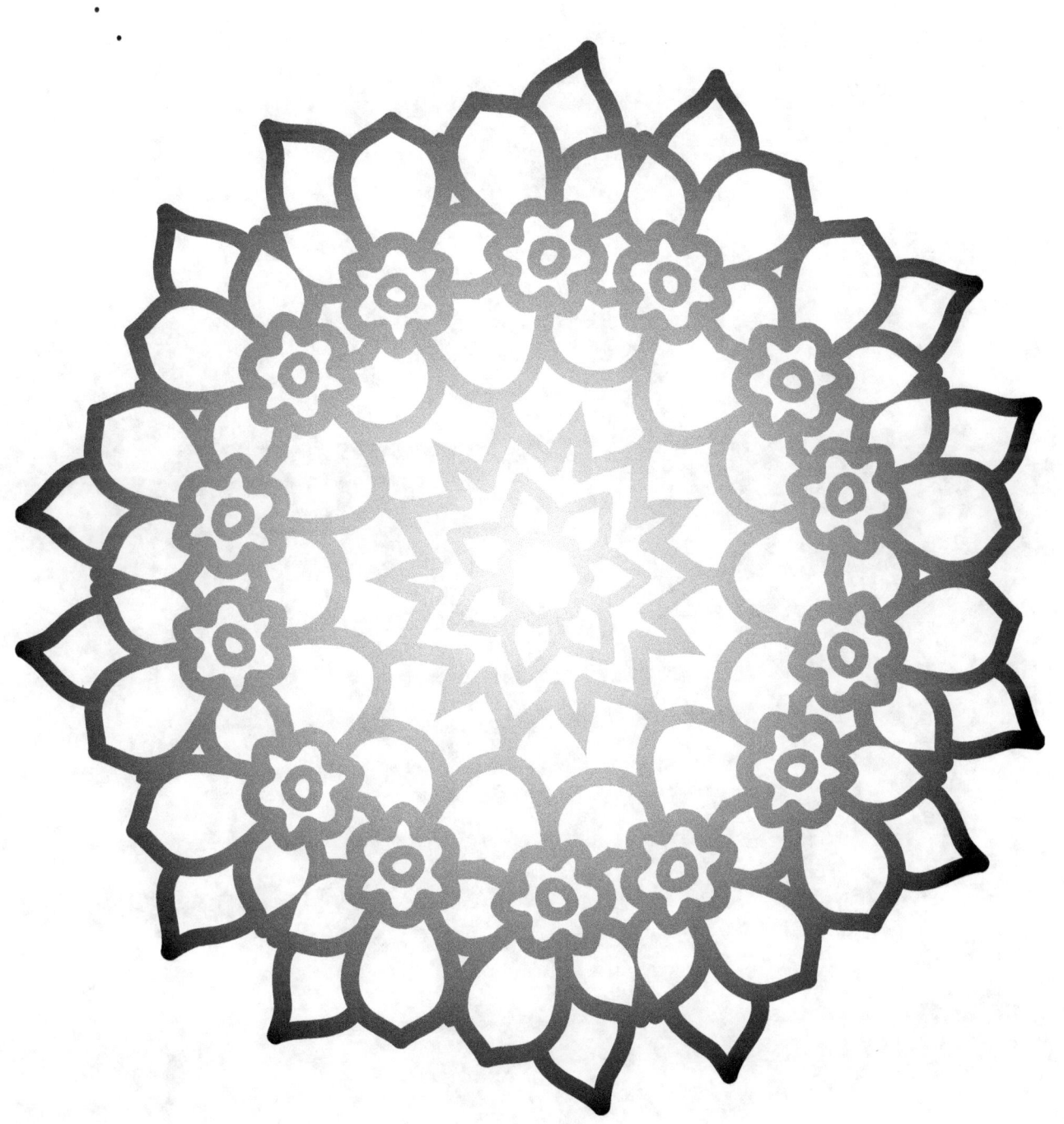

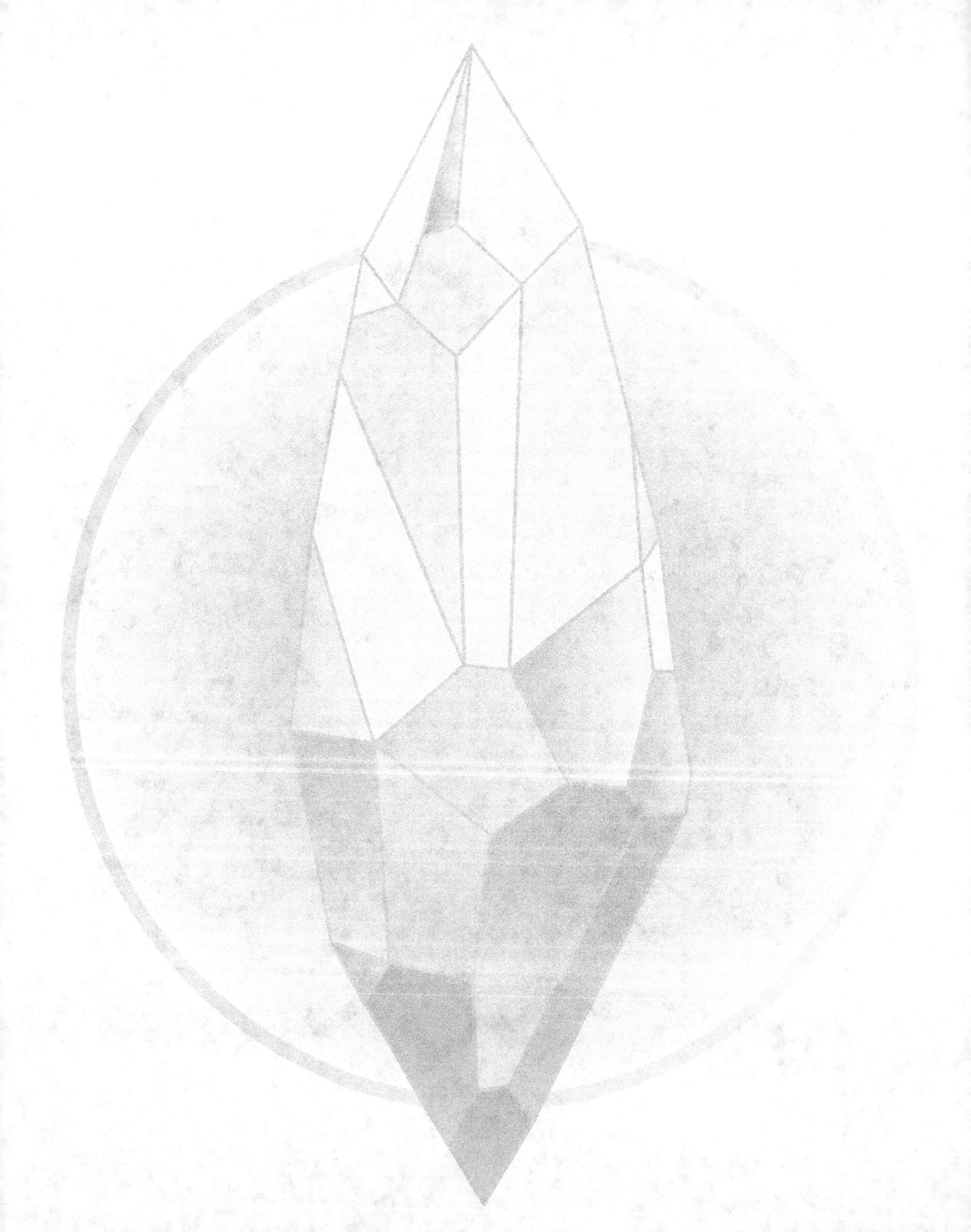

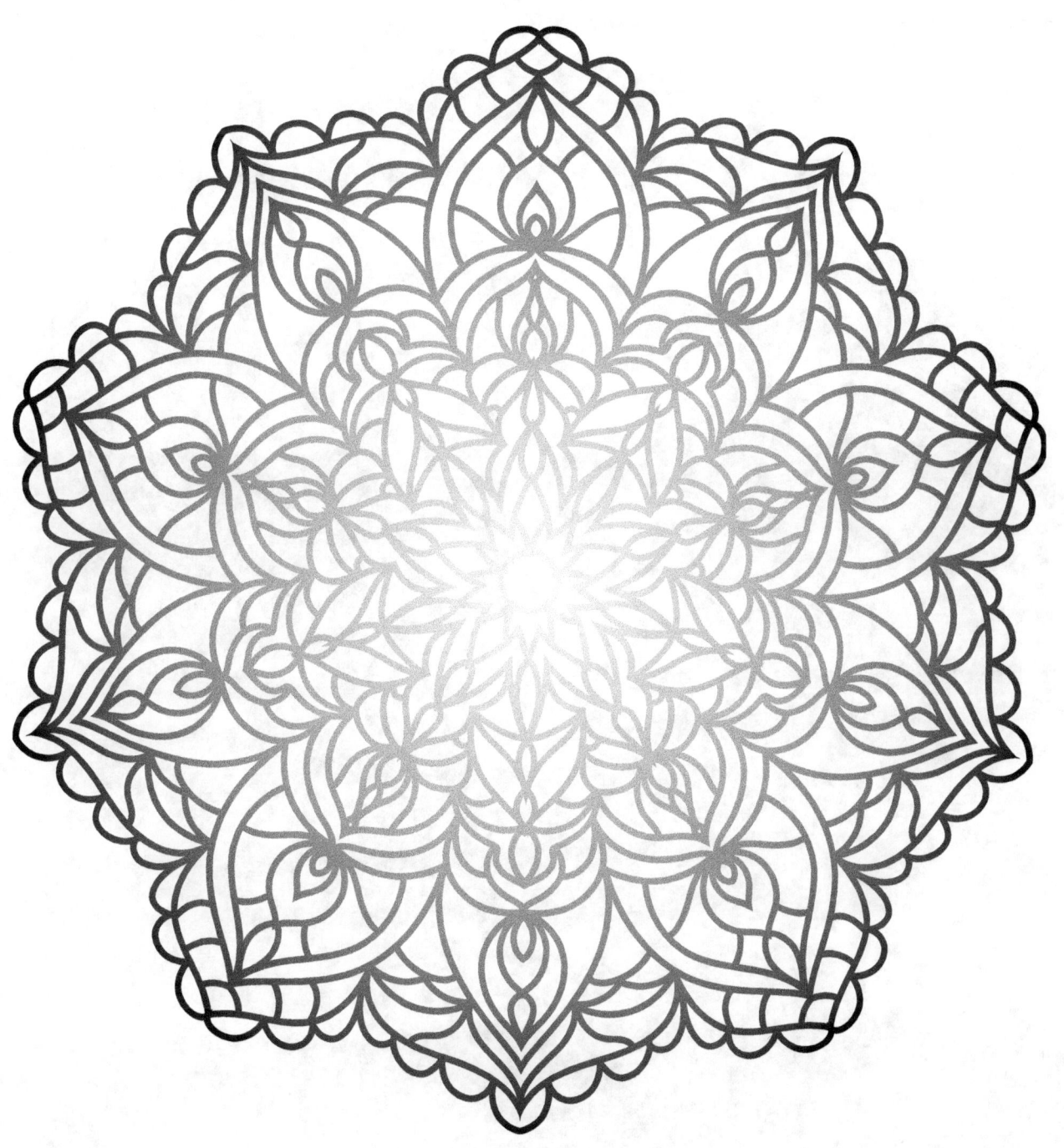

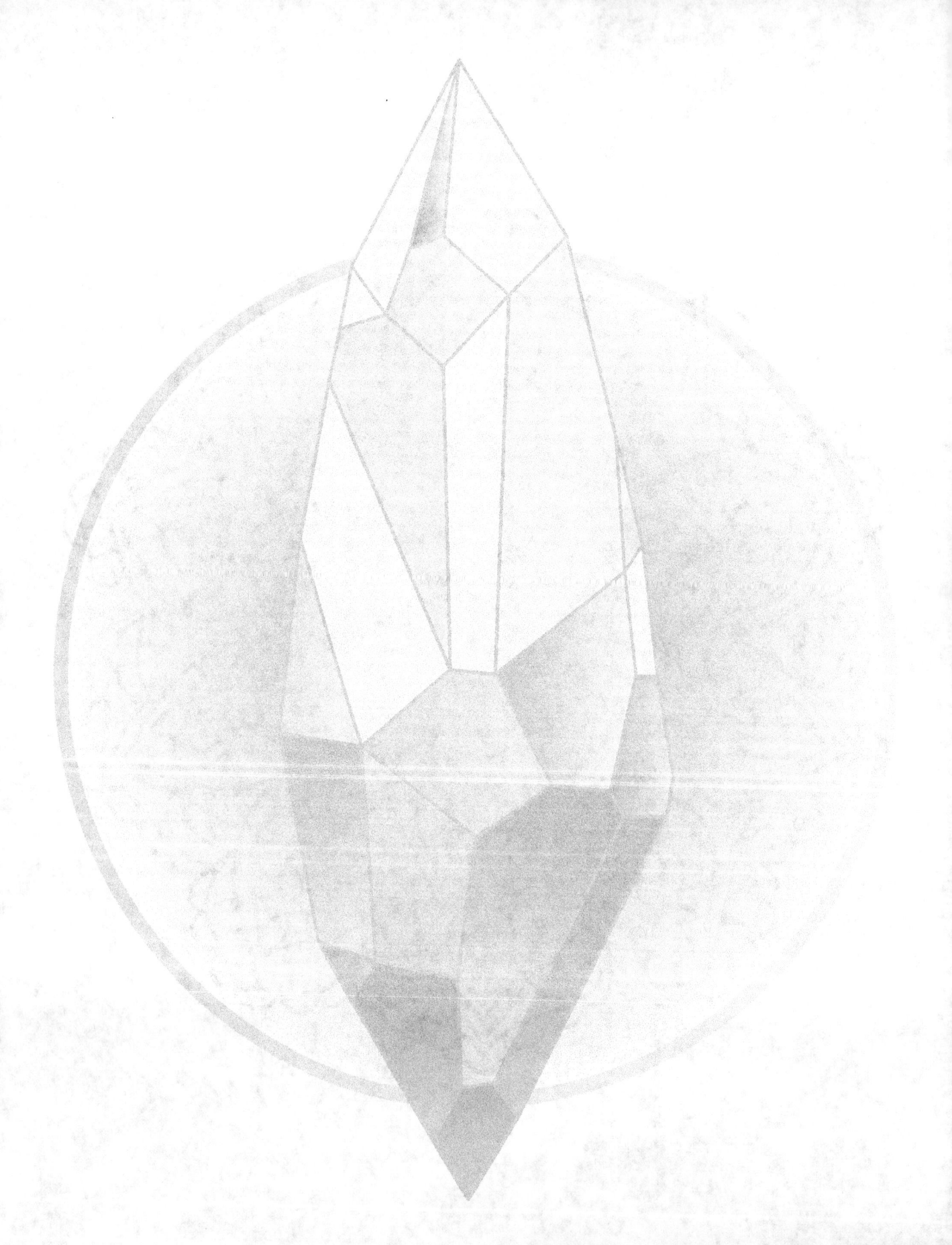

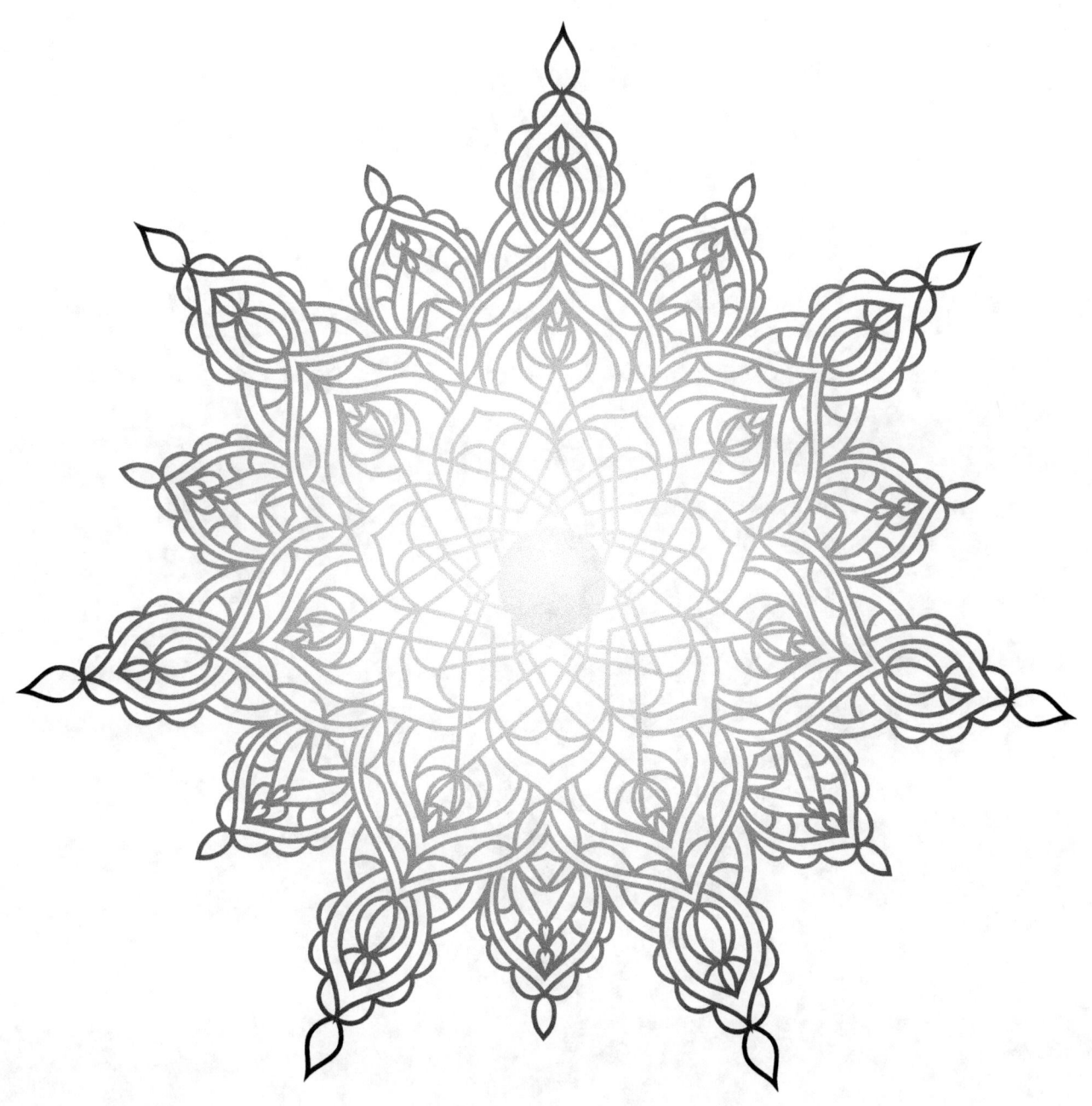

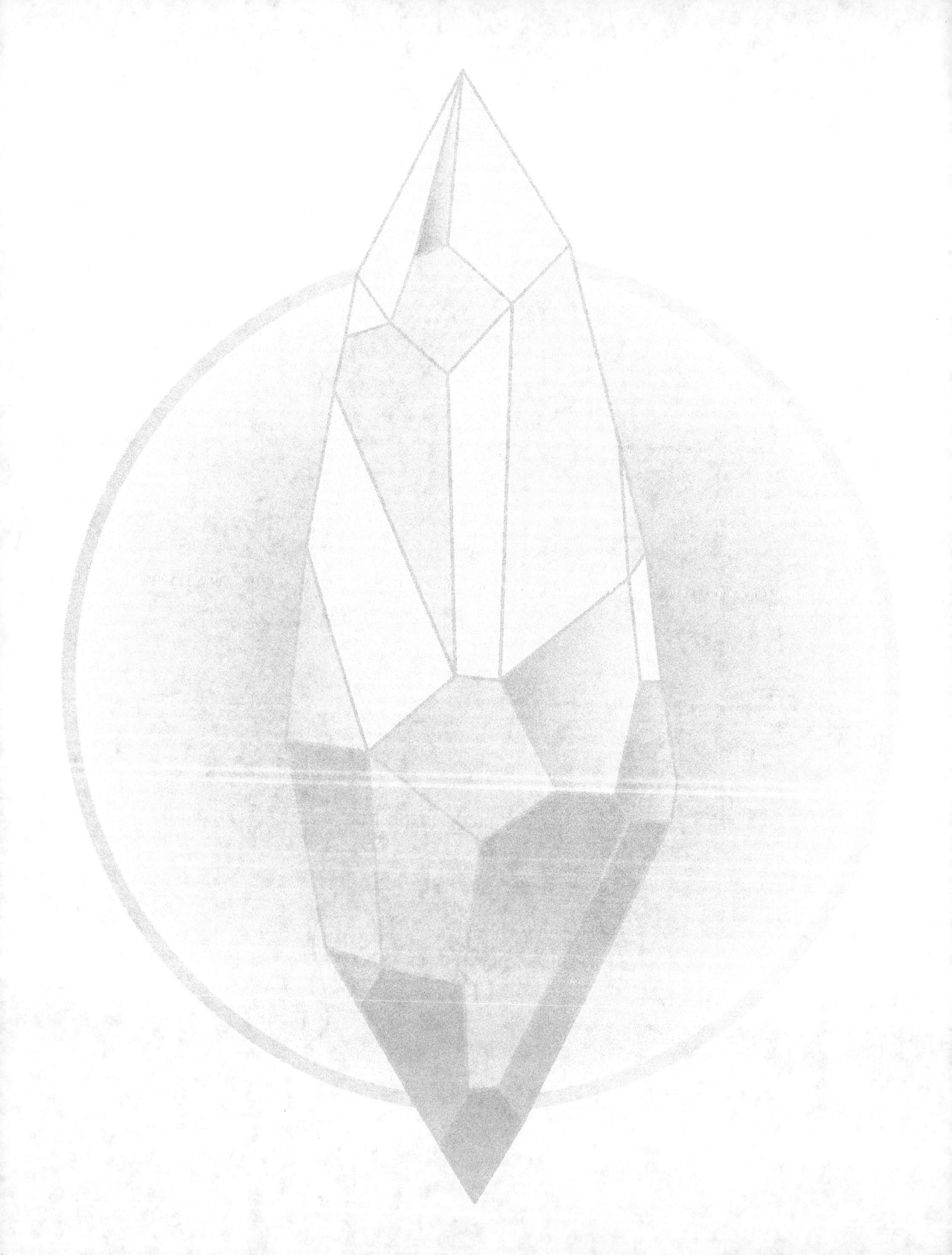

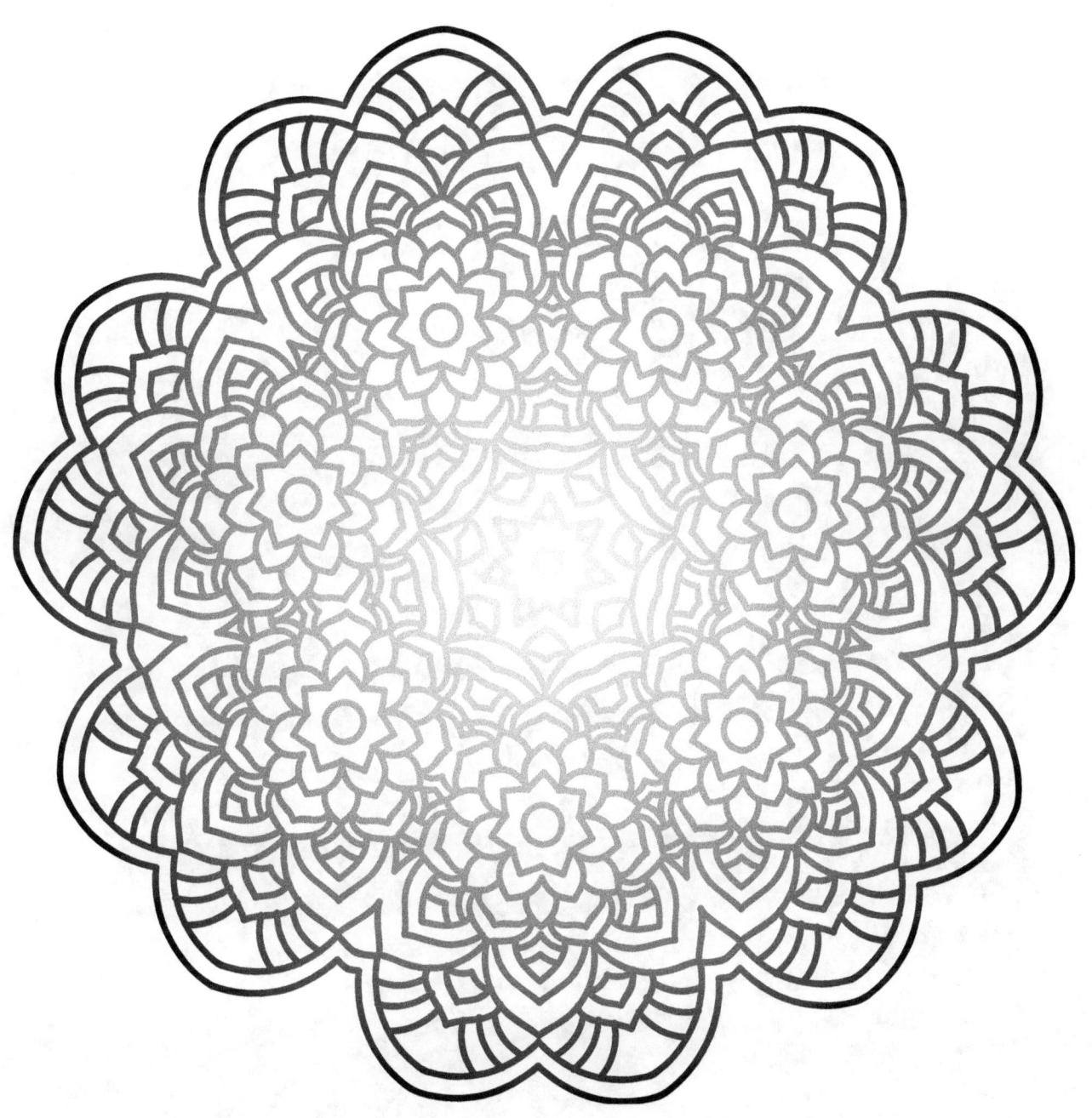

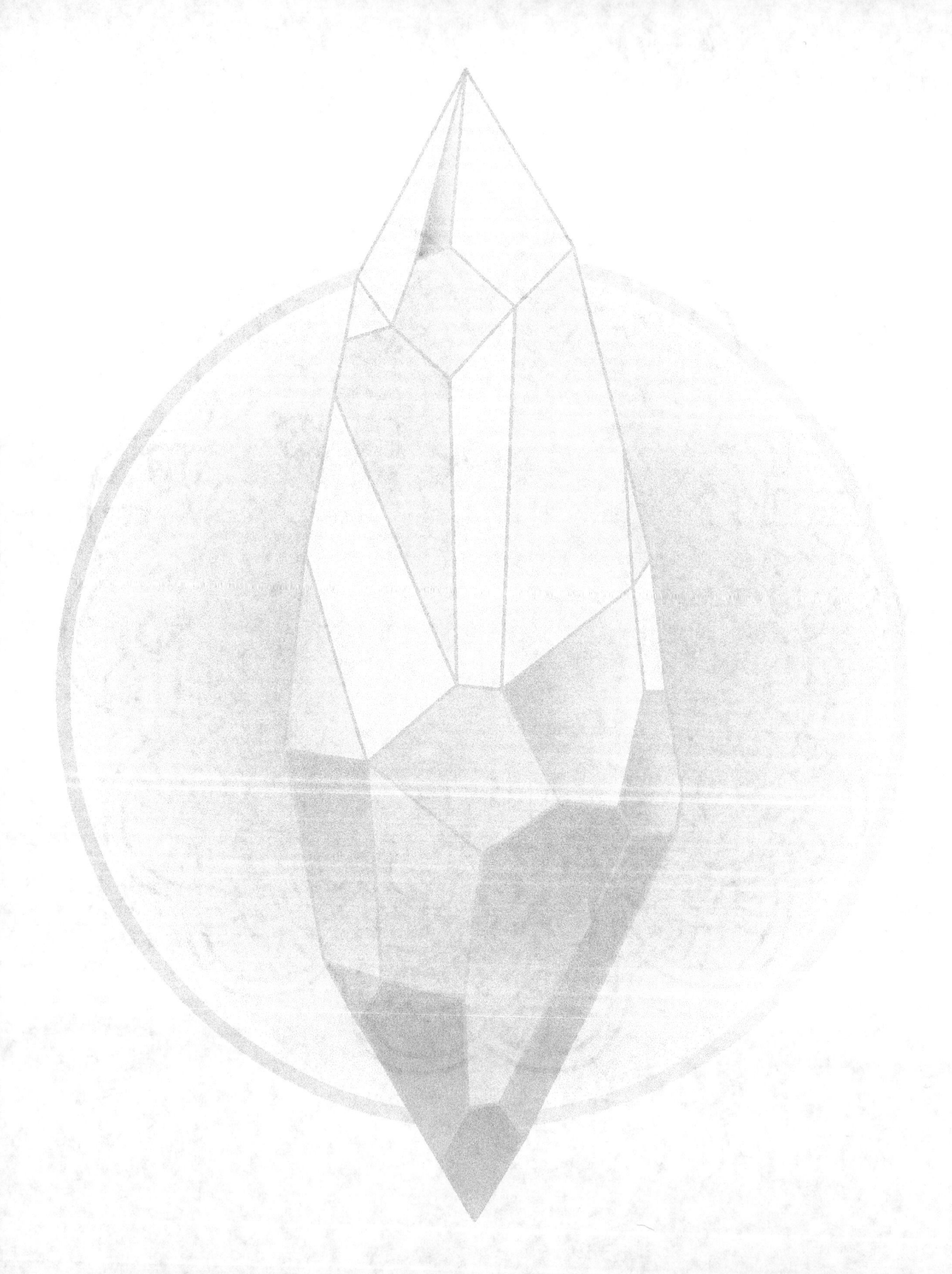

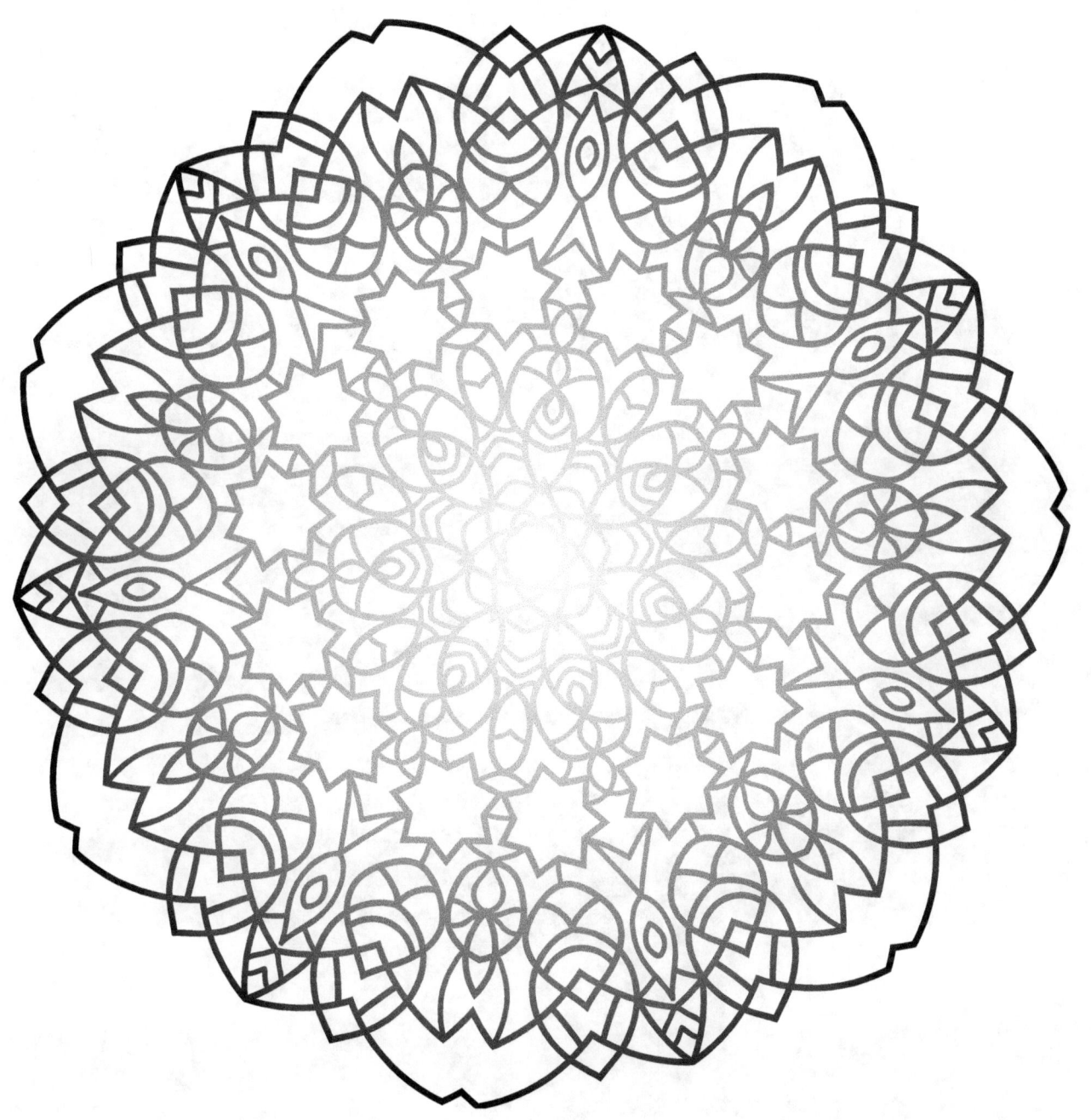

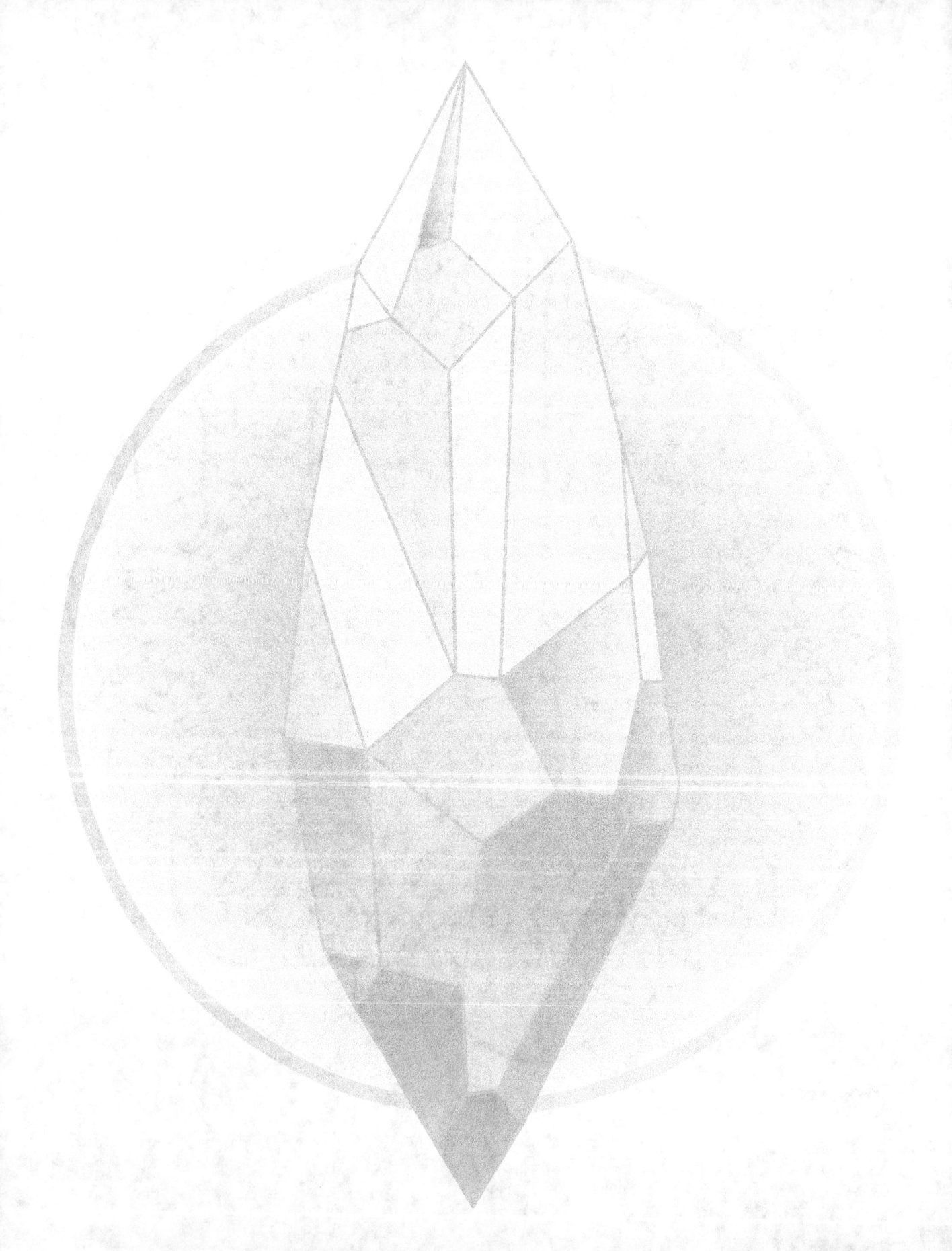

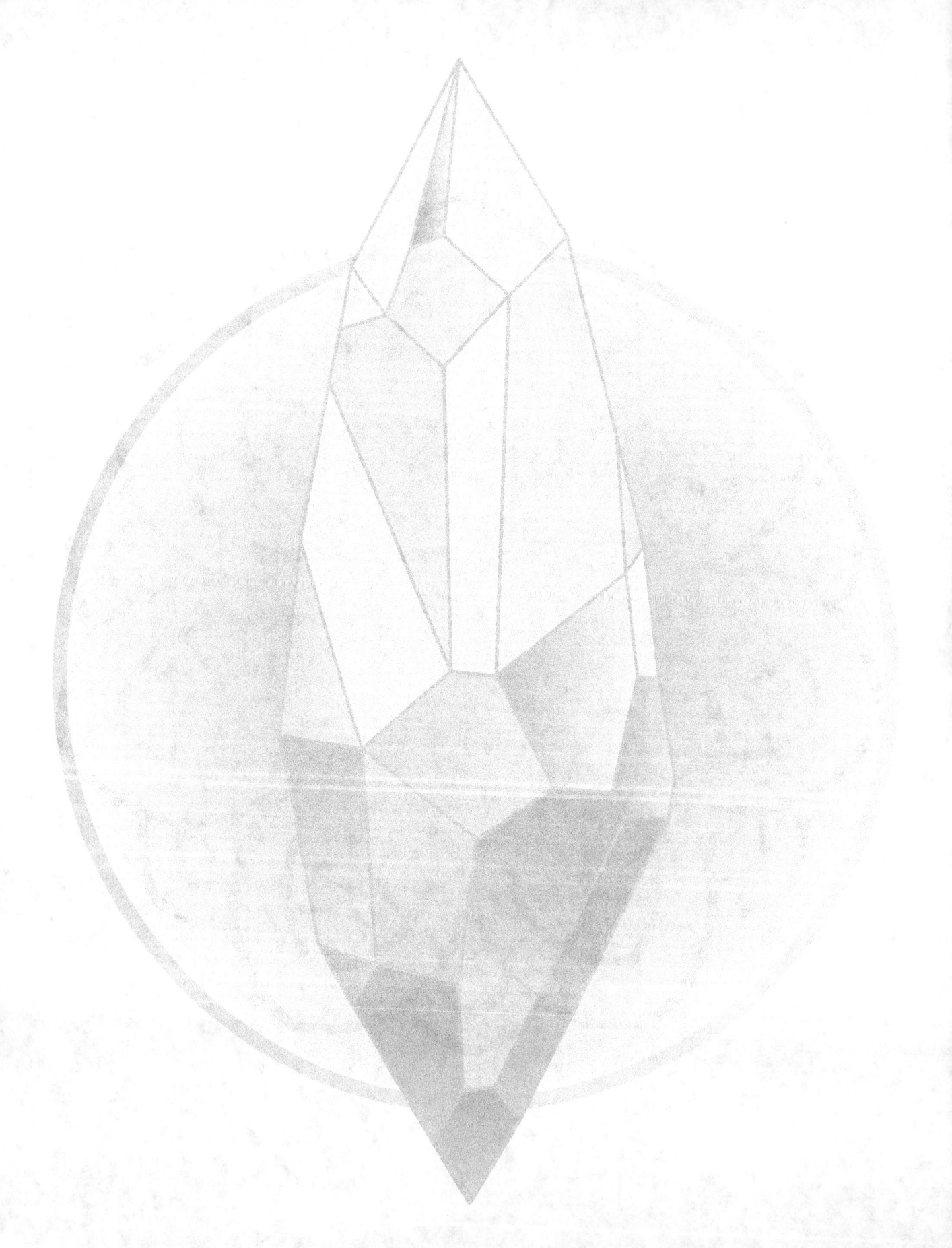

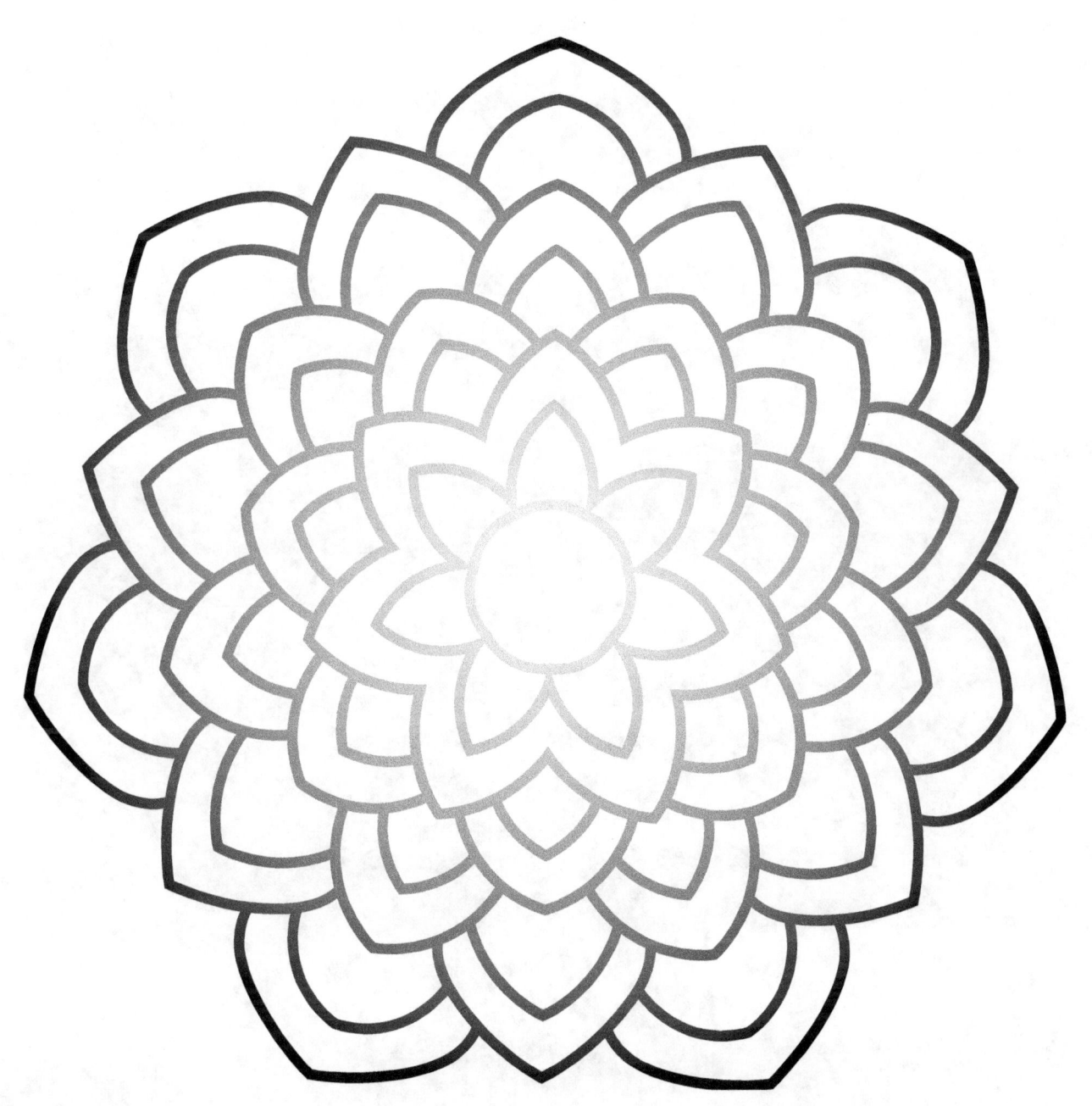

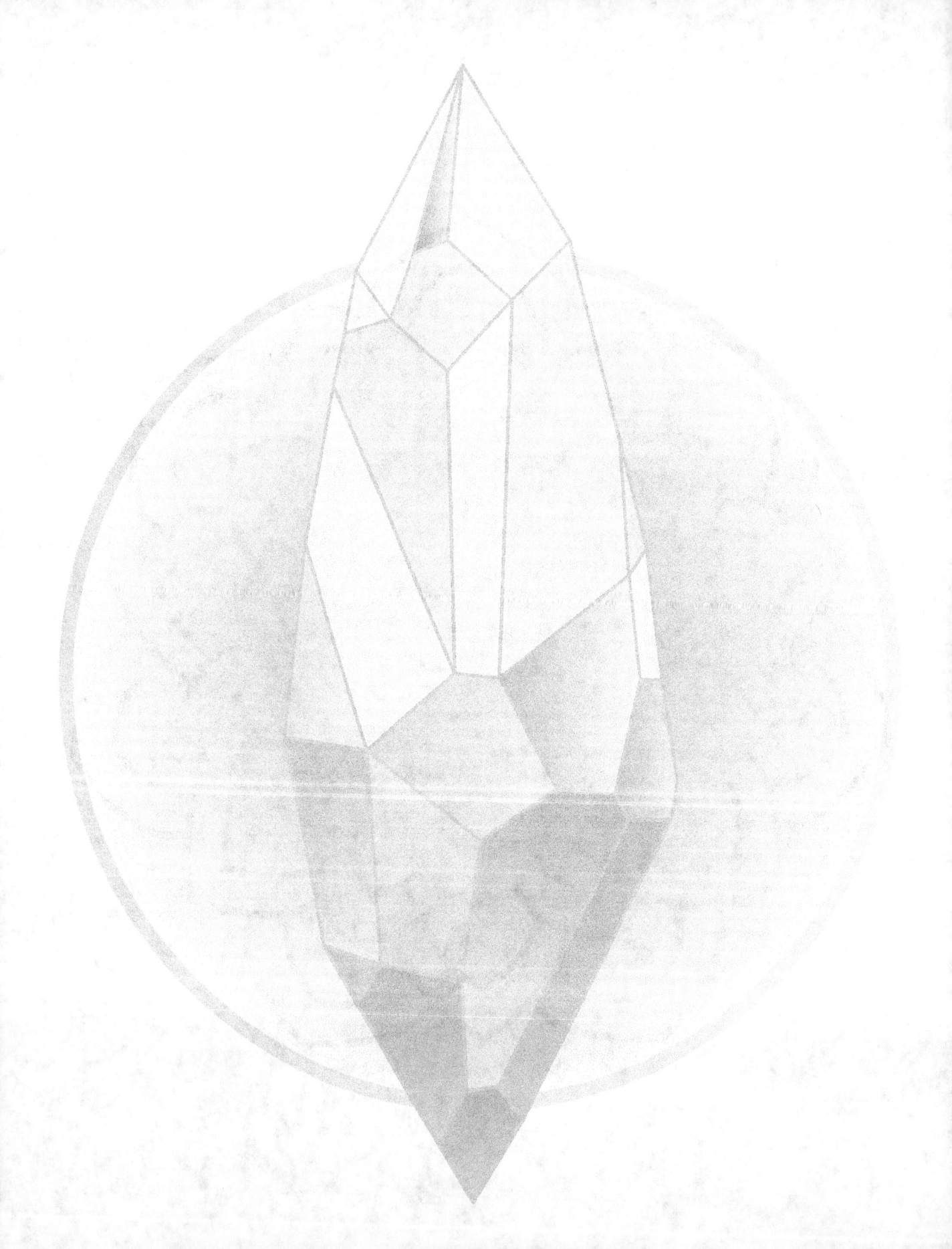

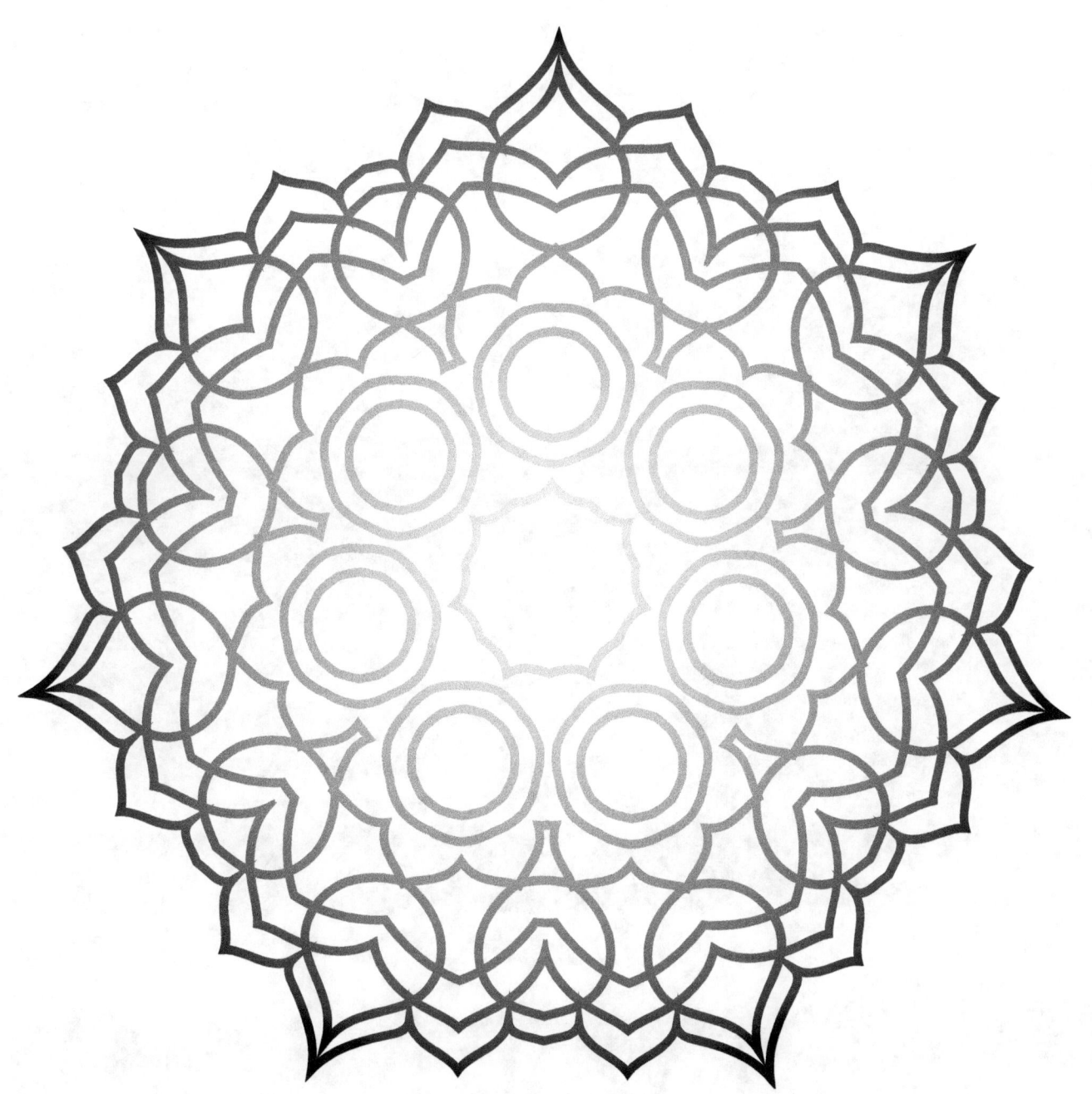

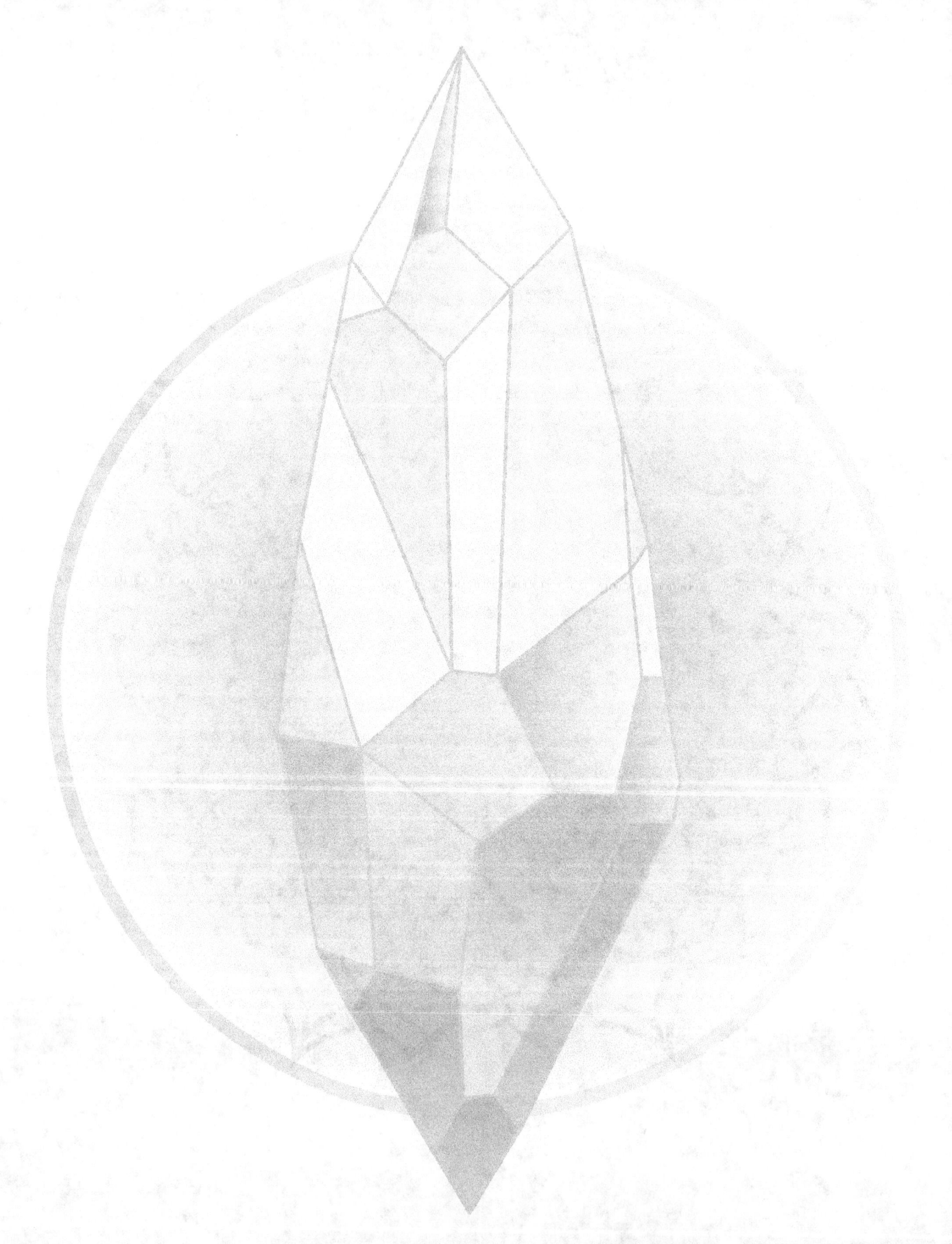

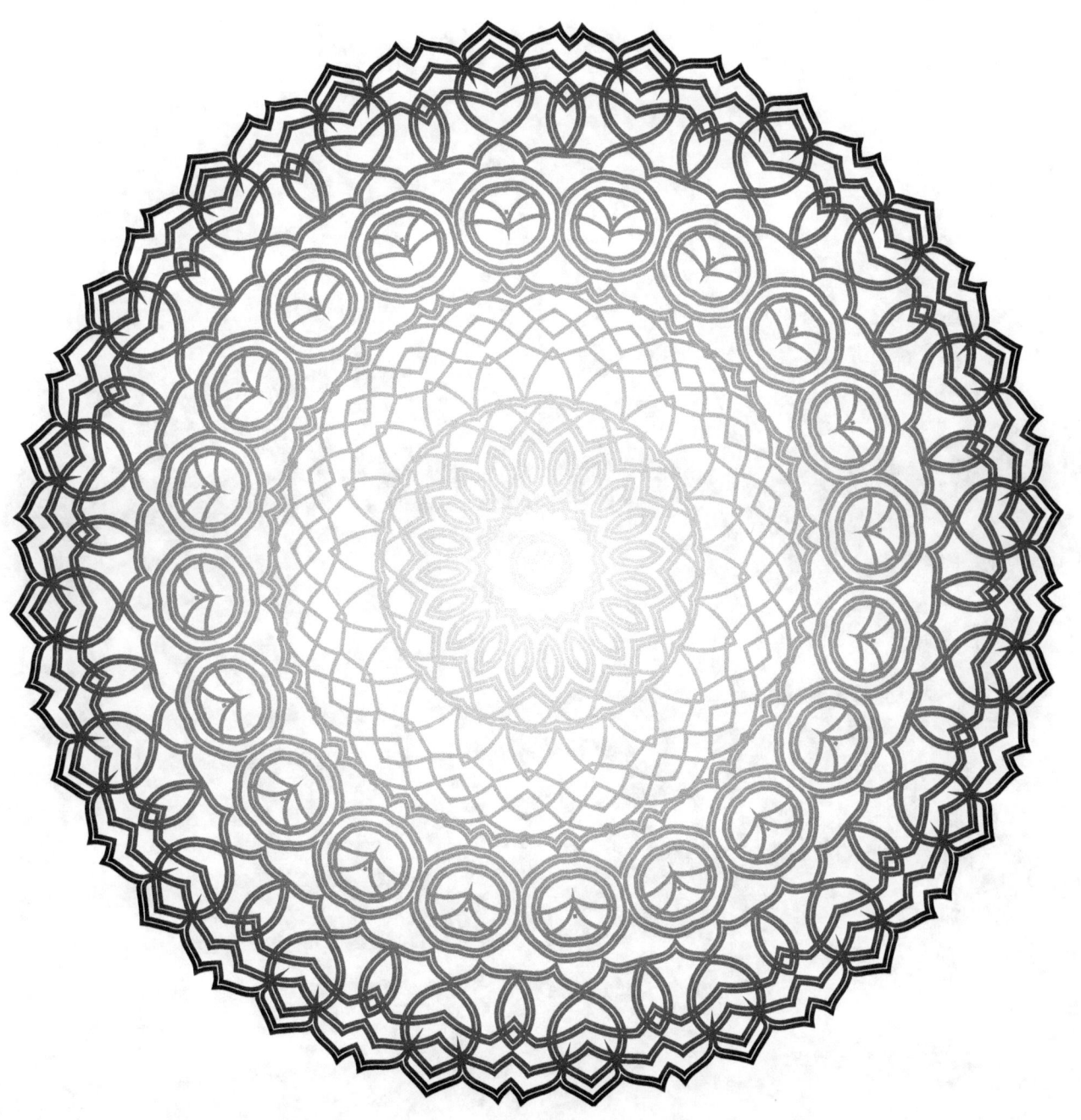

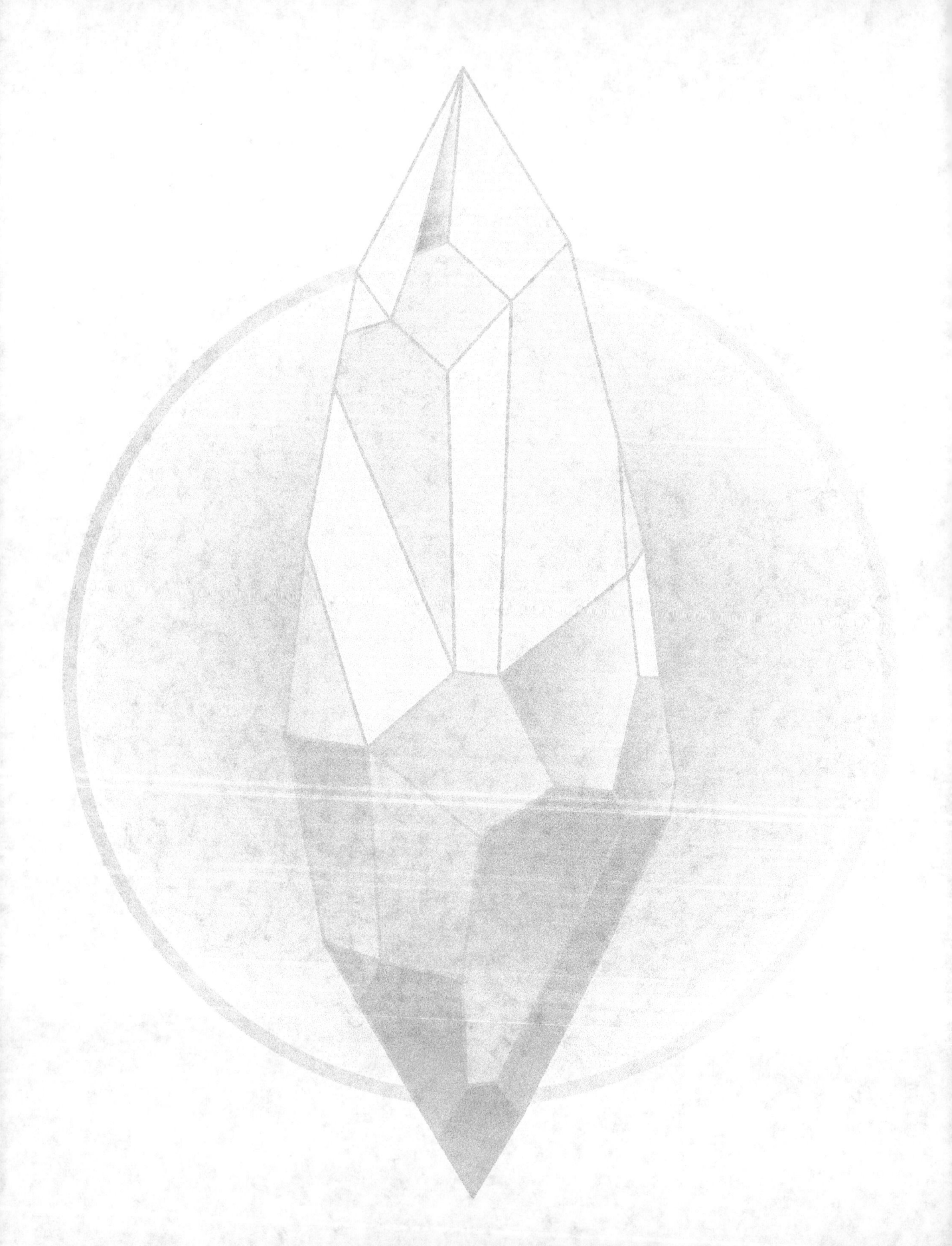

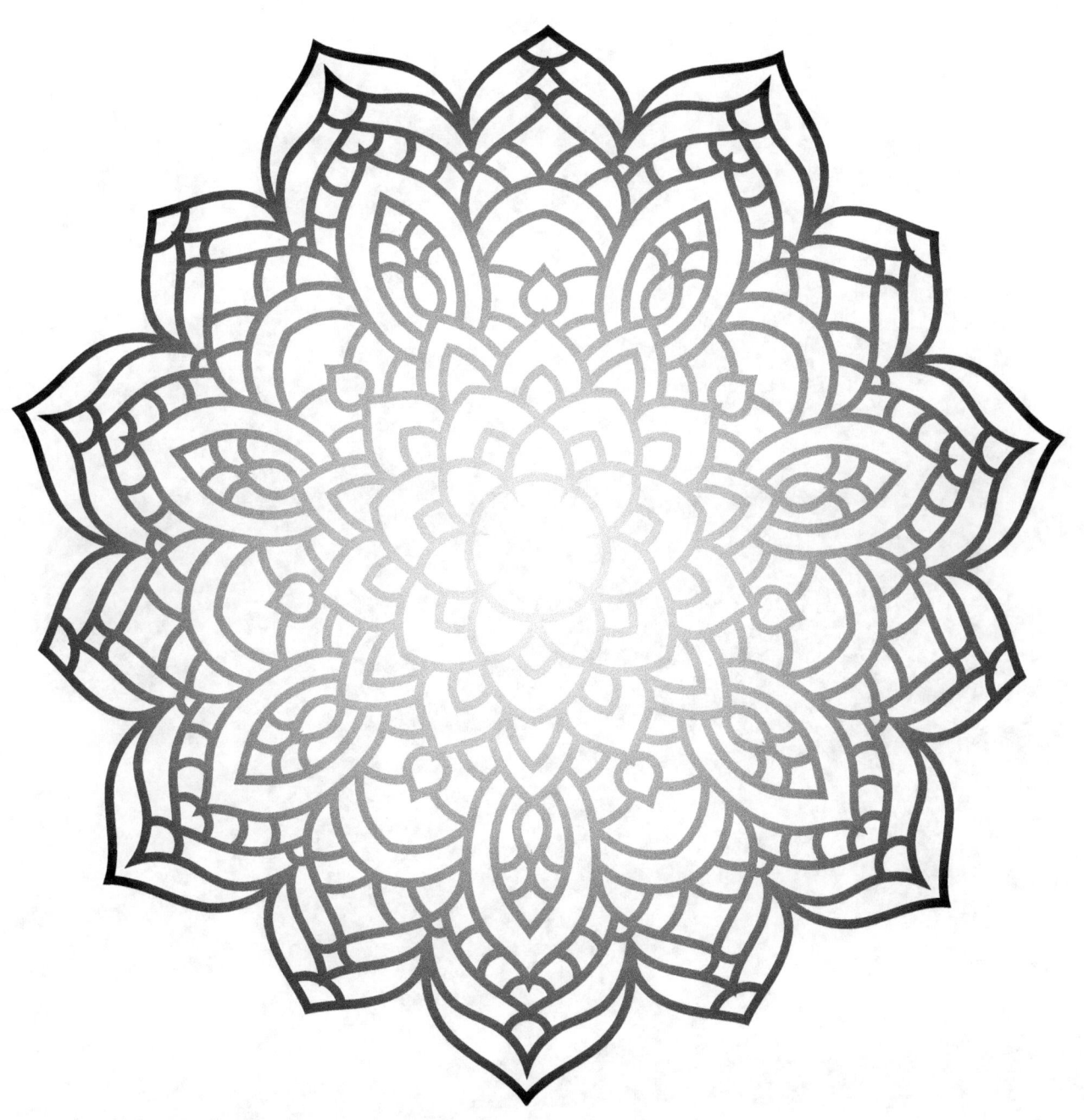

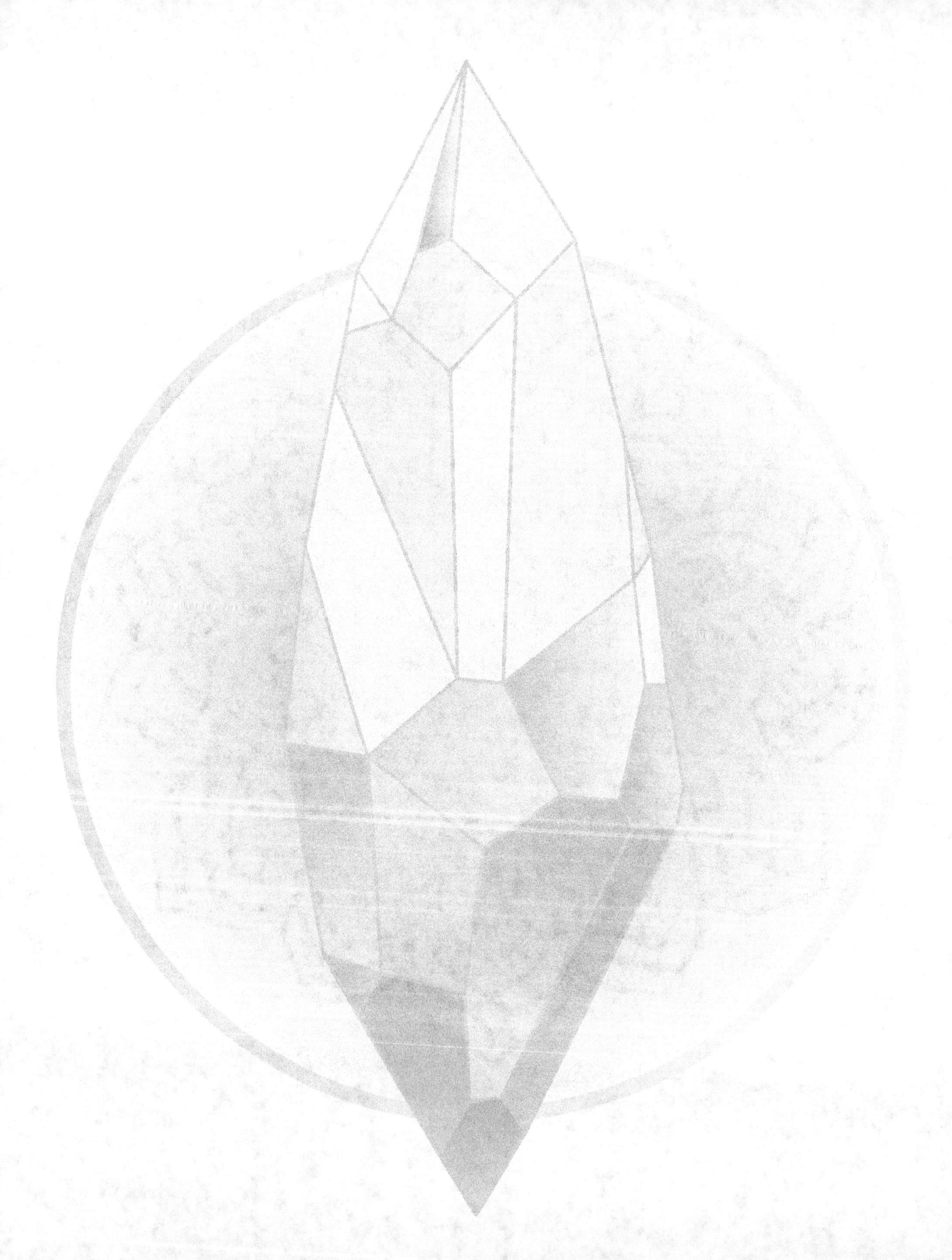

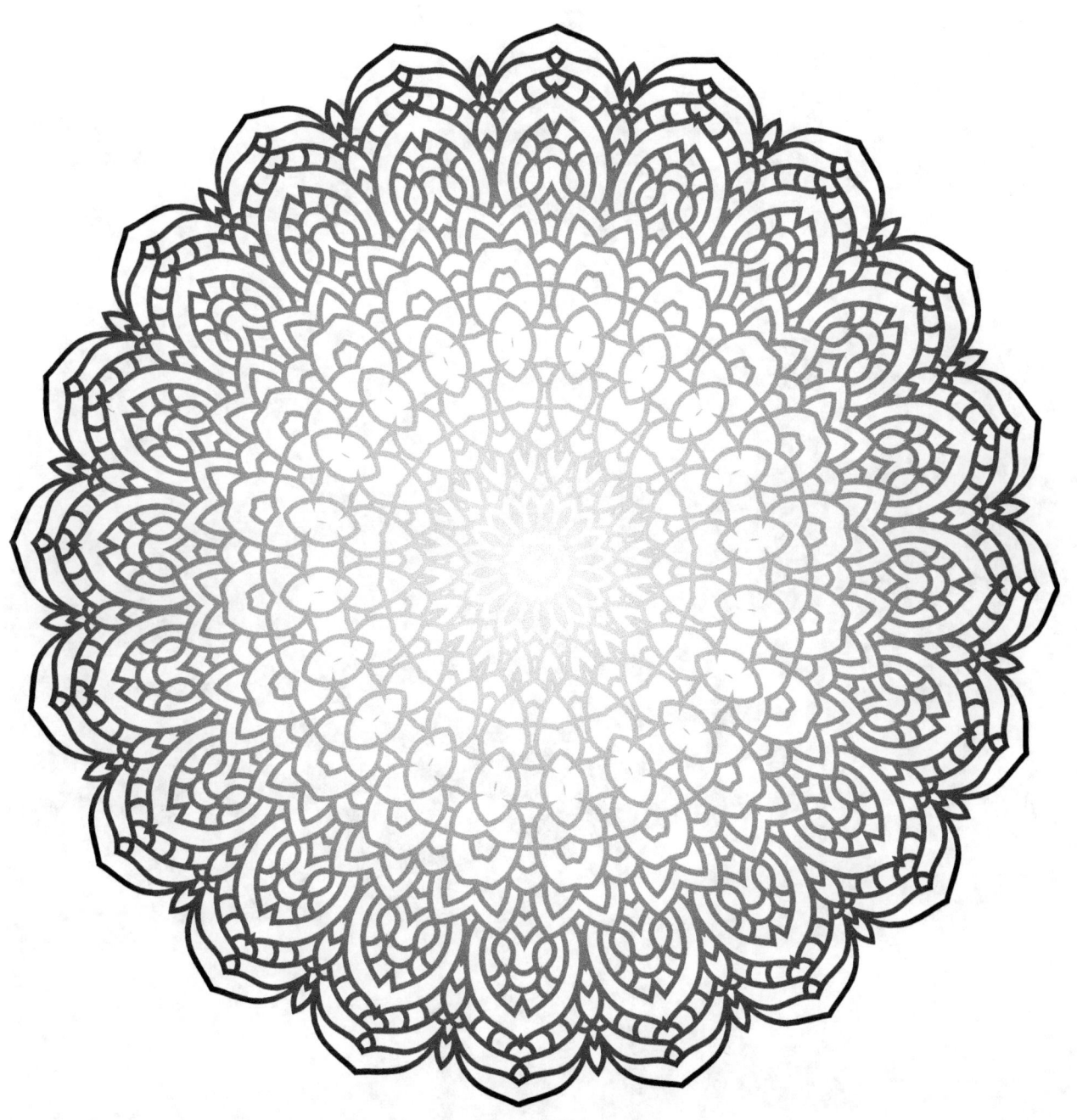

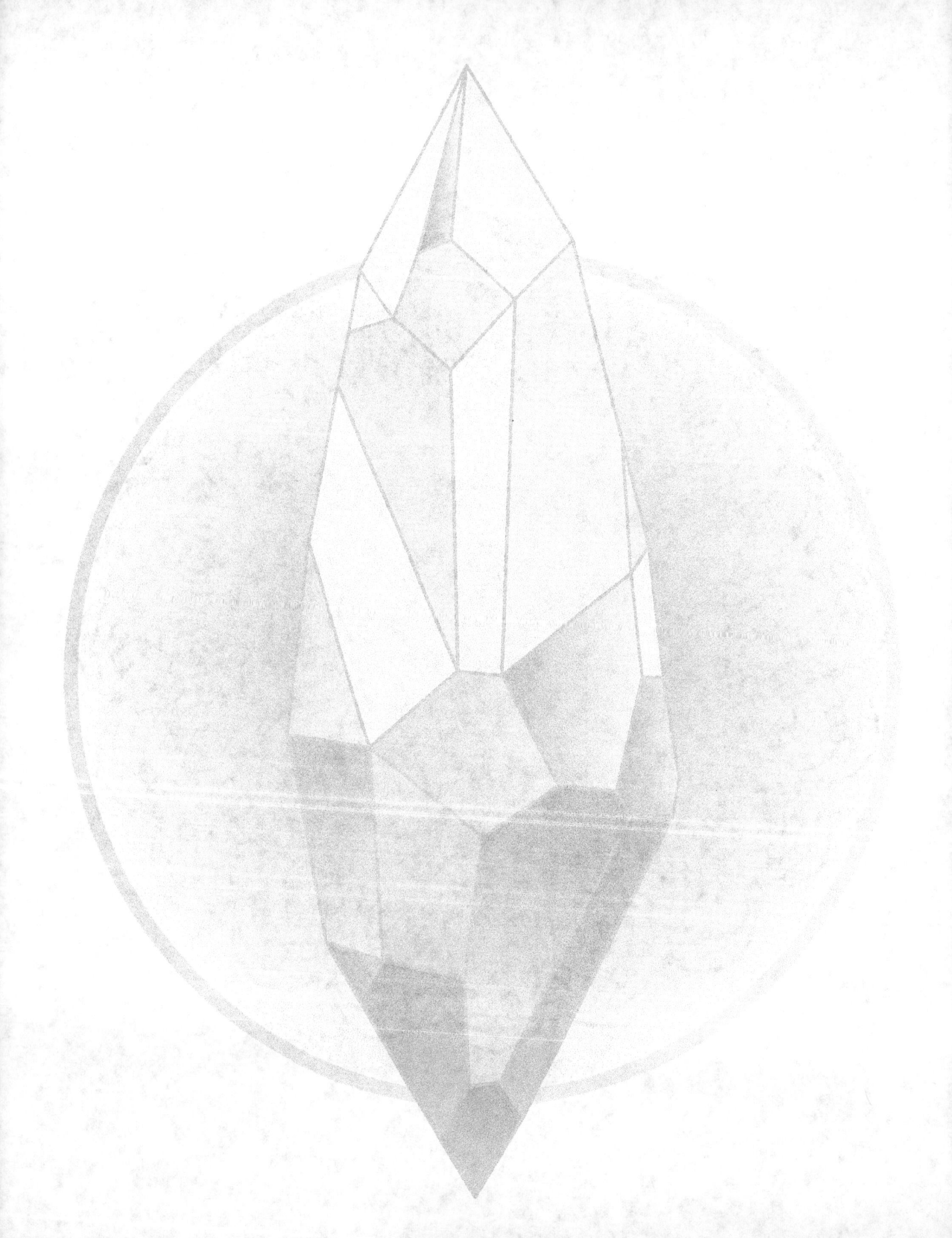

COLOR TEST PAGE

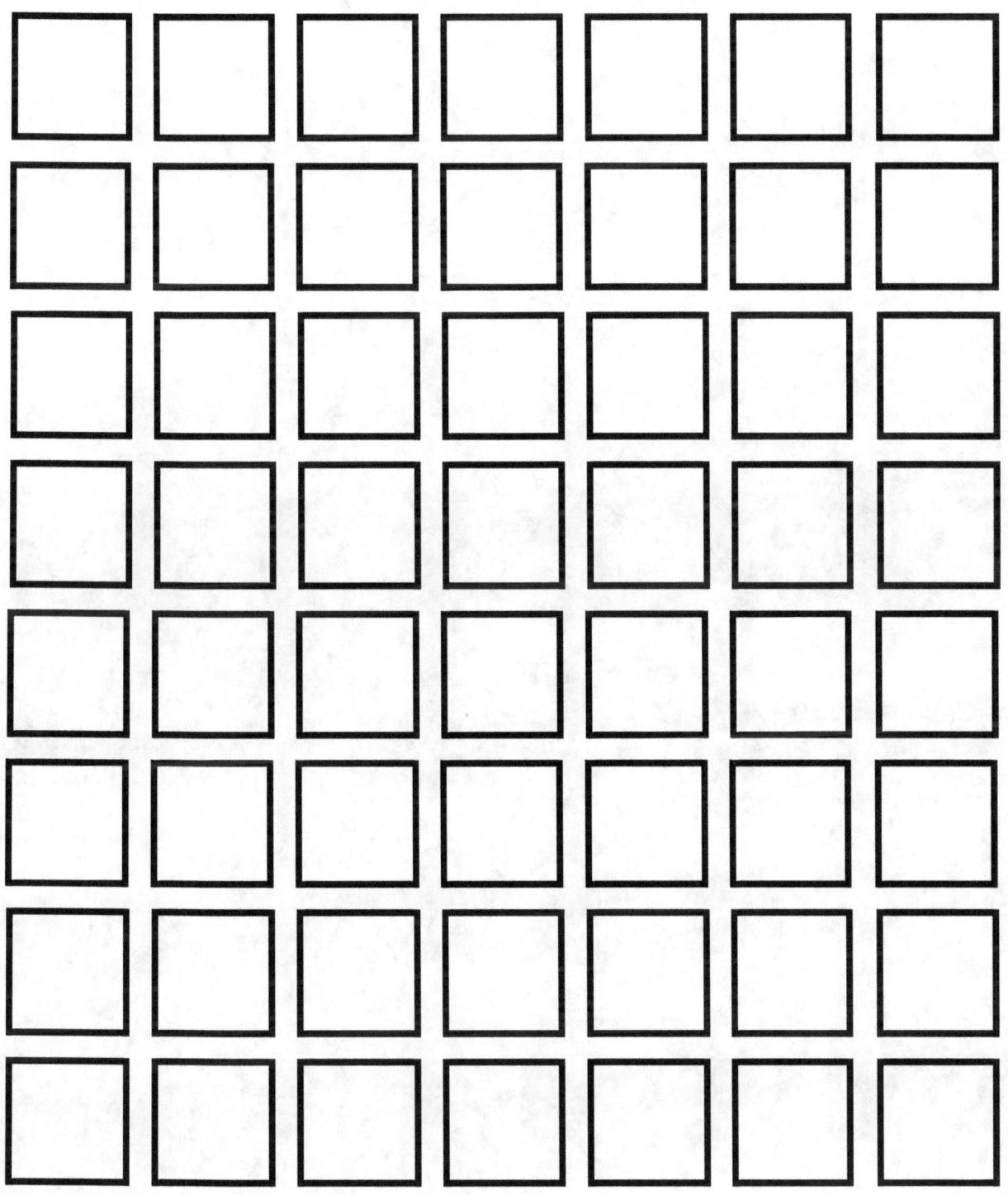

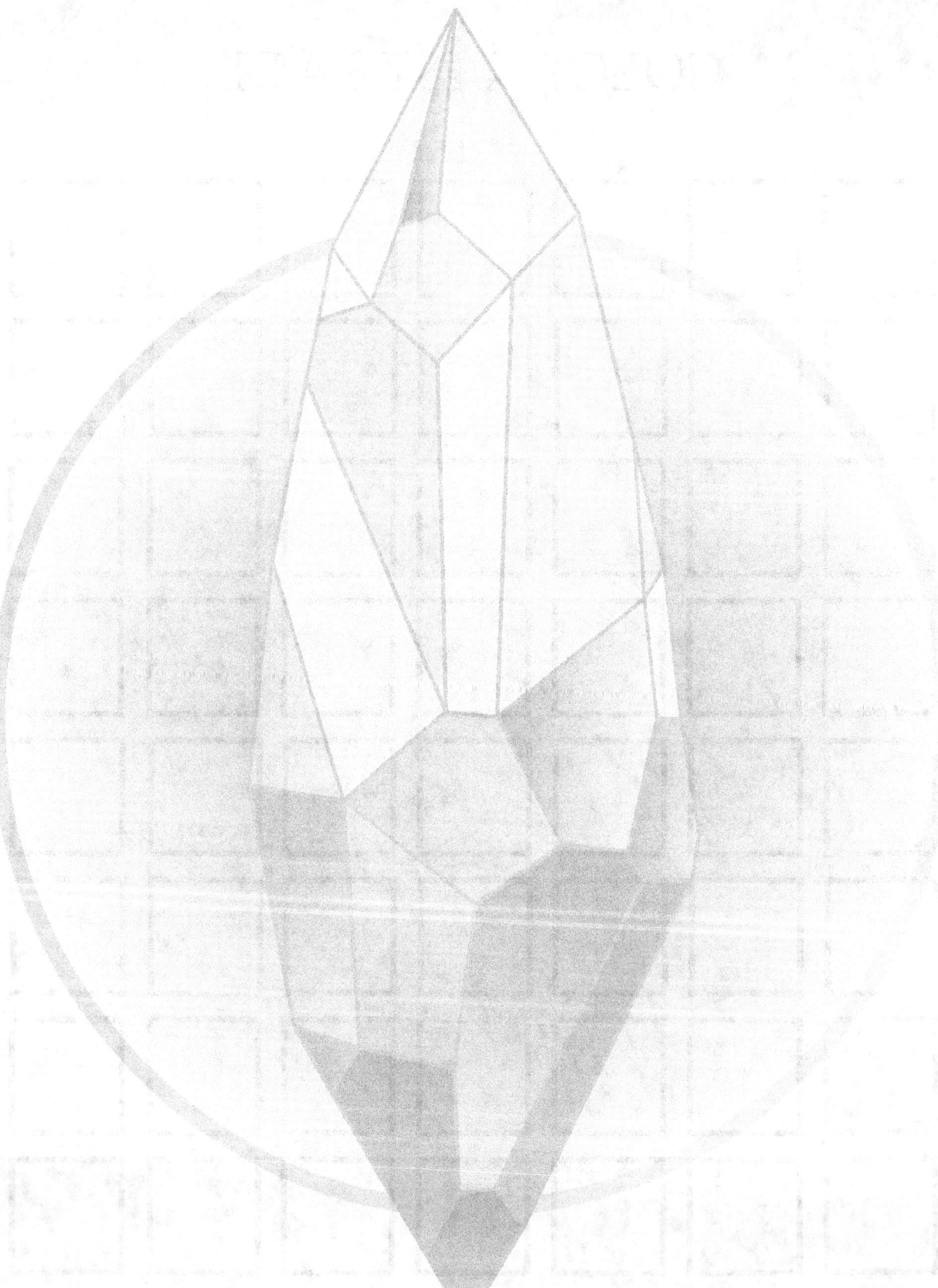

COLOR TEST PAGE

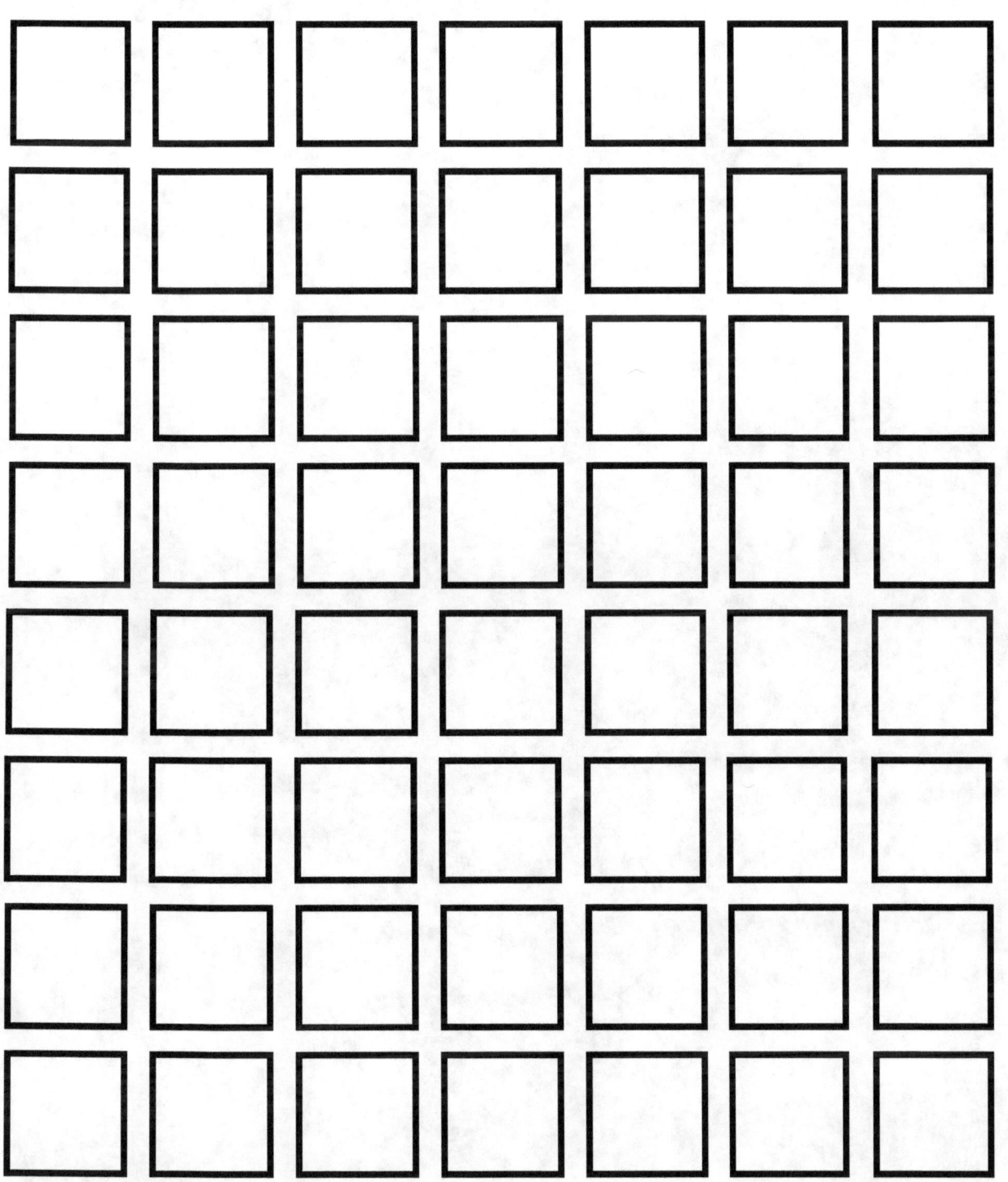

www.ingramcontent.com/pod-product-compliance
Lightning Source LLC
Chambersburg PA
CBHW081015170526
45158CB00010B/3047